Colorful
Crochet

THERESE HAGSTEDT

T S

TRAFALGAR SQUARE
North Pomfret, Vermont

First published in the United States
of America in 2015 by
Trafalgar Square Books
North Pomfret, Vermont 05053

Originally published in Swedish as
Colorful crochet.

ISBN: 978-1-57076-713-5

Library of Congress Control Number:
2015945031

TEXT AND PHOTOGRAPHY:
Therese Hagstedt
ILLUSTRATIONS: Jan Jäger
GRAPHIC DESIGN AND CAMERA COPY:
Petra Setterberg, www.petrasetterberg.se
EDITORS: Heidi-Maria Wallinder and
Roger Carlson
TRANSLATOR: Carol Huebscher Rhoades

Printed in China

10 9 8 7 6 5 4 3 2 1

DOESN'T COLOR MAKE EVERYONE HAPPY? I feel unbelievably happy when I see certain color combinations and I feel like a kid in a candy store whenever I buy yarn. Crochet is a great hobby for me, with all the wonderful colors and the chance to create something of my own. As a bonus, it is a type of therapy for the soul.

I've tried almost every craft one can do by hand: knitting, embroidery, weaving, and many others. But I became seriously attached to crochet several years ago, when I finally learned how to do it properly. I love all the possibilities crochet has to offer and, at the same time, its simplicity. It is easy and fun to crochet. Of course, one can choose to do complicated projects, but, for this book, I've limited myself to simple patterns.

Study the crochet basics at the beginning of this book if you haven't crocheted before. The only thing you need is a crochet hook and some yarn. When you feel more confident, you can begin to improvise.

There are patterns in the book for items you can crochet to make your home a more colorful place, for example, pillows, throws, and potholders. You will also find pretty accessories for your wardrobe: hats, shawls, slippers, bags, and much more. If you'd rather crochet something for a little one, you can choose between sweet garments, pennants, mobiles, and stuffed animals. One chapter is filled with decorations for the just right Christmas feeling. You can also create your own personal style with crocheted accessories in your favorite colors. These are guaranteed to elicit admiration—and I promise that no one will have the same things as you.

GOOD LUCK WITH YOUR CROCHETING AND HAVE FUN!

Contents

Learn to Crochet

Slip Knot

All crochet begins by making a slip knot. Work as follows:
1. Make a loop with the yarn's short end lying under the long end. **2.** Slide the long end under the loop and catch it with the crochet hook. **3.** Hold the yarn ends and draw the hook up so that the knot tightens. Now you can begin to crochet.

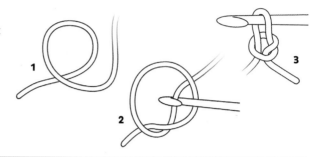

Chain Stitch (ch)

1. Beginning at the loop on the hook, wrap the yarn around the hook (see picture).
2. Bring the yarn through the loop on the hook. Repeat Steps 1-2 until you have the desired number of chain stitches.

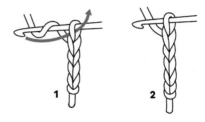

Single Crochet (sc; British double crochet, dc)

1. After working a chain of the desired number of stitches, insert the crochet hook into the second chain from the hook. **2.** Yarn around hook and through the stitch—you now have 2 loops on the hook. **3.** Yarn around the hook and through both loops on the hook. Now continue making a single crochet in each chain.

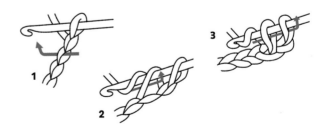

Half Double Crochet (hdc; British half treble, htr)

1. After working a chain of the desired number of stitches, wrap the yarn around the hook. Insert hook into the third chain from the hook. **2.** Yarn around the hook and through the chain stitch (there are now 3 loops on the hook). **3.** Yarn around the hook and through all three loops on the hook. **4.** Now one loop remains on the hook. Continue making a half double crochet in each chain.

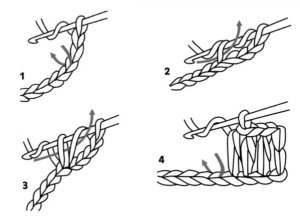

Double Crochet (dc; British treble, tr)

1. After working a chain of the desired number of stitches, wrap the yarn around the hook. Insert hook into the fourth chain from the hook. **2.** Yarn around the hook and through the chain stitch (there are now 3 loops on the hook). **3.** Yarn around the hook and through the first two loops on the hook. **4.** Yarn around the hook and through the remaining two loops on the hook. Only one loop remains on the hook. **5.** Now continue making a double crochet in each chain.

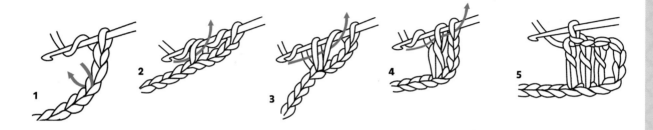

Treble Crochet (tr; British double treble, dtr)

1. Work as for a double crochet but begin with wrapping the yarn twice around the hook. Insert the hook into the fifth chain from the hook. **2.** Yarn around hook and through the chain stitch (there are now 4 loops on the hook).Yarn around hook and through the first two loops on the hook. **3.** Yarn around hook and through two loops on the hook. **4.** Finish with yarn around hook and through the remaining two loops on the hook. Only one loops remains on the hook. **5.** Now continue making a treble crochet in each chain.

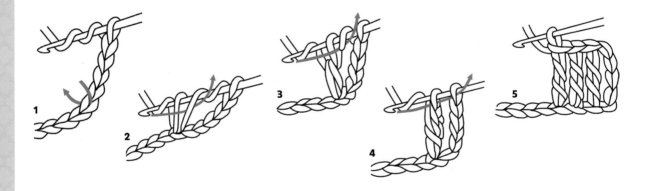

Slip Stitch (sl st)

Insert the hook through a stitch on the previous row and yarn around hook. Bring the yarn through both the stitch and the loop on the hook.

Chain Loop (ch loop)

A chain loop is made with two or more chain stitches, one after the other. It might be used, for example, between single, half double, double, or treble crochet stitches.

Double Crochet Group (dc gr)

Double crochet groups consist of several double crochet stitches made in the same stitch or around the same chain stitch loop. A double crochet group might also have chain stitches between each double crochet.

Stitch (st)

Round (rnd)

Repeats

Pattern repeats are usually placed within parentheses. For example: (2 dc, ch 1, 2 dc) 6 times means that you work the sequence of stitches between the parentheses a total of 6 times. If the instructions say: (1 sc in each of next 5 sts, 2 sc in next st) across, it means that you work the sequence within the parentheses to the end of the row.

Unless otherwise specified, always work through both stitch loops of previous row/round.

Sometimes, to shorten the instructions, the pattern says, for example, 7 dc – it means that you should work 1 dc in each of the next 7 sts.

Granny squares

Granny squares can be made in endless variations, not just in what you can do with them, but also how they look. I have tested many different styles but, in the end, most liked the ones my Aunt Lisbeth suggested. The reason I like this particular version is that you don't have to crochet any chain stitches between the double crochet groups along the sides and the square is tighter and firmer than other versions I've tried. Test it out—it's easy as can be once you try.

1. Work 4 ch.

2. Join chain into a ring with 1 sl st into the 1st ch st.

3. Rnd 1: Ch 3 (= the 1st dc), 2 dc around ring, (ch 1, 3 dc) 3 times, ch 1, and end with 1 sl st into top of ch 3. Cut yarn and draw end through last loop/stitch.

4. Change colors. **Rnd 2:** Insert hook under last chain loop and bring yarn through. Now you have 1 sl st around the ch loop.

5. Ch 3, 2 dc, ch 1, 3 dc around the 1st ch loop. (Skip 3 dc and, around next ch loop, work 3 dc, ch 1, 3 dc) around. End by skipping 3 dc and then work 1 sl st into top of ch 3 at beginning of rnd. Cut yarn and draw end through last st if you want to change colors.

6. The square now has 4 groups of (3 dc, ch 1, 3 dc).

7. Rnd 3: With a new color, bring up the yarn between dc groups at the middle of one side. Ch 3, 2 dc in the center space. *Skip 3 dc and work (3 dc, ch 1, 3 dc) around the ch loop in the corner. Skip 3 dc and work 3 dc in the next center space. Continue repeating from * to the end of the rnd and finish as for Step 5.

8. The square looks like this after Rnd 3 is completed.

9. Continue building the square round after round with (3 dc, ch 1, 3 dc) at each corner and 3 dc groups in each space between corners.

10. Continue as set, making the square bigger and bigger on every round until it is the size you want. Now the square is finished and you can weave in all the yarn ends neatly on the wrong side.

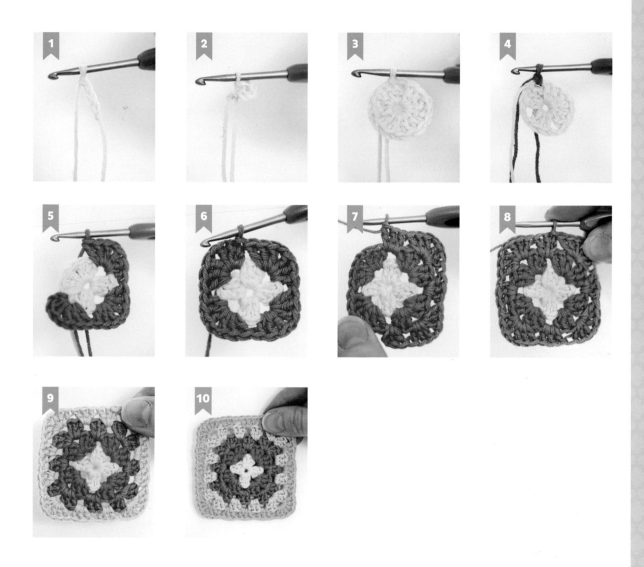

There are many different ways to join granny squares. Once you've finished crocheting all the squares for a project, you can decide whether to sew or crochet them together. A little further along in the book, I will explain several ways to crochet the finished squares together. A very neat way to join the finished squares, which I prefer, is to crochet the squares together as you make them. It is so much fun to see the piece grow as the squares are joined. Here's a description of the method I use:

1. Crochet a complete square. Work the next square through the second-to-last round. Begin the last round as usual until you reach the side where the squares will be joined.

2. At this point, you would normally work (3 dc, ch 1, 3 dc) in the corner. To join, work the 3 dc as usual, but, instead of ch 1 between the dc groups, insert the hook into the corresponding ch loop (at the corner) on the square that is already finished. Yarn around hook and through the loop, yarn around hook again and through (as for 1 sc). Now continue by working 3 dc in the same corner.

3. Use the same method in the 3 dc group along the side. Insert the hook into the space between the dc groups on the finished square. Yarn around hook and through the loop, yarn around hook again and through (as for 1 sc). Continue, working 3 dc in the next space of the half-finished square.

4. This is how the squares look when they've been joined along one side.

5. When you are joining four squares and are at a corner, insert the hook and draw up the yarn through each of the 3 corners. You should have 4 loops on the hook before you wrap the yarn around hook and draw it through all 4 loops at the same time.

6. After completing the corner, continue joining the squares as previously.

A Little Extra for Decoration

IN THIS CHAPTER, YOU'LL find sweet little things that you can use to decorate almost anything that needs a spark of color. Flowers, butterflies, and hearts are simple, small projects that don't take much time to make once you've learned how. They are rather habit-forming once you've started. These projects provide an excellent way to use up your leftover yarns. Use the yarns you have on hand and choose a crochet hook size that works for those yarns. If you want a looser flower, use a larger size hook; if you want a firmer one, choose a smaller hook. Try it out!

Flowers in several layers

FLOWER IN SEVERAL LAYERS WITH A "WHEEL" AT THE CENTER

These flowers have become my signature, the two favorites I often use to decorate hats and other items. The flower petals are crocheted in several layers, but you can decide how many to use and which size you want. Both flowers are crocheted following the same basic method; only the center part is different. Instructions for the second variation are on page 20.

Yarn: CYCA #1 (sock/fingering/baby) Mandarin Petit (100% cotton, 195 yd/178 m / 50 g; *see page 142*)
Crochet Hook: U.S. size D-3 / 3 mm

1. Ch 4.
2. Join into a ring with 1 sl st into 1st ch.
3. Ch 4 (= the 1st dc + 1 ch), (1 dc around ring, ch 1) 5 times; end with 1 sl st into 3rd ch at beginning of round.
4. Ch 1, 1 sc around next ch loop, (ch 3, 1 sc around next ch loop of previous rnd) 5 times; end with ch 3 and 1 sl st into 1st ch at beginning of rnd. There should now be 6 ch-3 loops = Rnd 2.
5. Make the petals around the flower. Work (1 sc, ch 1, 3 dc, ch 1, 1 sc) in each ch loop around. End with 1 sl st into the 1st sc. Cut yarn and draw end through last st.
6. Change colors. Turn the flower so wrong side (WS) is facing. Insert the hook into the 2nd rnd and work 1 sc around the petal as shown in the photo.

7. Ch 4, (1 sc in the 2nd rnd and around next petal, ch 4) 5 times; end with 1 sl st into the 1st sc at beginning of rnd = Rnd 4.
8. There should now be 6 ch-4 loops.
9. Turn the flower with right side (RS) facing. Work (1 sc, ch 1, 4 dc, ch 1, 1 sc) in each ch loop around. End with 1 sl st into the 1st sc. Cut yarn and draw end through last st.
10. Change colors. Turn the flower with the WS facing. Insert the hook into the 4th rnd and work 1 sc.
11. Ch 5 and then work 1 sc around next sc of previous rnd. Continue the same way around until there are a total of 6 ch loops; end with 1 sl st into 1st sc.
12. Turn flower with RS facing. Work (1 sc, ch 1, 5 dc, ch 1, 1 sc) in each ch loop around. Cut yarn and draw end through last st. Fasten off ends or continue to add layers, alternating flower petals and ch loops, increasing 1 ch st in each ch loop and 1 dc in each petal on every repeat.

When the flower is the desired size, cut yarn and draw end through last st. Weave in all ends neatly on WS.

FLOWER IN SEVERAL LAYERS WITH A SOLID CENTER

Yarn: CYCA #1 (sock/fingering/baby) Mandarin Petit (100% cotton, 195 yd/178 m / 50 g; *see page 142*)

Crochet Hook: U.S. size D-3 / 3 mm

Ch 4. Join into a ring with 1 sl st into 1st ch. End all rnds with 1 sl st into 1st st to complete the round.

Rnd 1: Ch 1, work 6 sc around ring.

Rnd 2: Ch 1, (work 2 sc) in each st around.

Rnd 3: Ch 1, 1 sc, (ch 3, skip 1 sc, 1 sc) 5 times; end with ch 3 and 1 sl st. There should now be 6 ch loops.

Rnd 4: Ch 1, work (1 sc, ch 1, 3 dc, ch 1, 1 sc) in each ch loop around.

Rnd 5: Turn so WS is facing. Ch 1, work (1 sc around sc on 3rd rnd (crochet around the stitch) and then ch 4) 6 times. End with 1 sl st into 1st sc at beginning of rnd. There should now be 6 ch-4 loops. Turn.

Rnd 6: Ch 1, work (1 sc, ch 1, 4 dc, ch 1, 1 sc) in each chain loop around. Cut yarn and draw end through last st or continue making more layers as for Rnds 5-6, increasing 1 ch st in each ch loop and 1 dc in each petal on every repeat. When flower is desired size, cut yarn and weave in ends neatly on WS.

A special but very decorative and fun flower that looks best when you crochet it with a slightly fluffy yarn.

Yarn: CYCA #3 (DK/light worsted) Sandnes Duo (55% Merino wool, 45% cotton, 136 yd/124 m / 50 g; *see page 142*)

Crochet Hook: U.S. size G-6 / 4 mm

Ch 4. Join into a ring with 1 sl st into 1st ch.

Rnd 1: Ch 1, work 10 sc around the ring and end with 1 sl st into 1st sc = 10 sts.

Rnd 2: Ch 1, work 2 sc in each st around; end with 1 sl st into 1st sc = 20 sts.

Rnd 3: Work (ch 12, 1 sl st into next st of the front ch loop) around.

Rnd 4: Work (ch 14, 1 sl st into next st of back ch loop) around.

Cut yarn, leaving a long tail, and draw end through last st. Use tail to sew the flower where you want. If you like, sew a button to the flower center.

Simple flowers

Simple flowers are exactly that, flowers worked in only one layer. They are lovely just as they are, but several can also be joined instead of crocheting one flower with several layers. Choose a size of flower that will go well with the item you wish to decorate.

SIMPLE FLOWER 1

Yarn: CYCA #1 (sock/fingering/baby) Mandarin Petit (100% cotton, 195 yd/178 m / 50 g; *see page 142*)
Crochet Hook: U.S. size D-3 / 3 mm

Ch 4. Join into a ring with 1 sl st into 1st ch. End all rnds with 1 sl st into 1st st to complete the round.
Rnd 1: Ch 1, work 12 sc around ring.
Rnd 2: Ch 1, (1 sl st, 3 dc in next st) 6 times. Cut yarn and draw end through last st. Weave in ends neatly on WS.

SIMPLE FLOWER 2

Yarn: CYCA #1 (sock/fingering/baby) Mandarin Petit (100% cotton, 195 yd/178 m / 50 g; *see page 142*)
Crochet Hook: U.S. size D-3 / 3 mm

Ch 4. Join into a ring with 1 sl st into 1st ch.
Rnd 1: Ch 2 (= 1 dc), work 11 dc around ring; end with 1 sl st into top of ch 2.
Rnd 2: Ch 1, (1 sc, 5 dc in next st) 6 times; end with 1 sl st into 1st ch.
Cut yarn and draw end through last st. Weave in ends neatly on WS.

SIMPLE FLOWER 3

Yarn: CYCA #1 (sock/fingering/baby) Mandarin Petit (100% cotton, 195 yd/178 m / 50 g; *see page 142*)
Crochet Hook: U.S. size D-3 / 3 mm

Ch 4. Join into a ring with 1 sl st into 1st ch. End all rnds with 1 sl st into 1st st to complete the round.
Rnd 1: Ch 1, work 6 sc around ring; end with 1 sl st into 1st ch.
Rnd 2: Ch 1, (2 sc in each sc) around = 12 sc.
Rnd 3: Ch 1, (1 sc in next sc, 2 sc in next st) 6 times = 18 sts.
Rnd 4: Ch 1, (1 sc in next st, 5 dc in next st) 9 times.
Cut yarn and draw end through last st. Weave in ends neatly on WS.

SIMPLE FLOWER 4

Yarn: CYCA #1 (sock/fingering/baby) Mandarin Petit (100% cotton, 195 yd/178 m / 50 g; *see page 142*)
Crochet Hook: U.S. size D-3 / 3 mm

Ch 5. Join into a ring with 1 sl st into 1st ch.
Rnd 1: Ch 2 (= 1 dc), 23 dc around ring; end with 1 sl st into top of ch 2 at beginning of rnd.
Rnd 2: Ch 4, skip 3 sts, 1 sc, (ch 3, skip 3 sts, 1 sc) 5 times and end with ch 3, 1 sl st into 1st of the ch 4 at beginning of rnd.
Rnd 3: Slip st to 1st ch loop, ch 3 (= 1 dc), 1 dc, ch 1, 2 dc in ch loop, work (2 dc, ch 1, 2 dc) in each of remaining 5 ch

loops; end with 1 sl st into top of ch 3 at beginning of
rnd.

Rnd 4: Slip st to ch of 1st dc group, ch 3 (= 1 dc), 6 around
ch in dc group, skip 2 dc, 1 sc between dc, (7 dc around ch
in dc group, skip 2 dc, 1 sc between dc) 5 times; end with
1 sl st into top of ch 3 at beginning of rnd. Cut yarn and
draw end through last st. Weave in ends neatly on WS.

Coiled flowers

These pretty coiled flowers are crocheted in a long spiral, coiled into a flower shape and then sewn together with a few stitches. What about adding a bead to the center? Here are various sizes of flowers.

SMALL COILED FLOWER *(Photo 1, page 25)*

Yarn: CYCA #1 (sock/fingering/baby) Mandarin Petit (100% cotton, 195 yd/178 m / 50 g; *see page 142*)

Crochet Hook: U.S. size D-3 / 3 mm

Ch 27.

Row 1: Skip 4 ch and work 1 sc into 5th ch from hook, (ch 2, skip 1 st, 1 sc) to end of chain; turn.

Row 2: Work 1 sc, ch 1, 3 dc, ch 1, 1 sc in each ch-2 loop of previous row. Cut yarn and draw end through last st. Coil the spiral into a flower shape (see photo) and use a few stitches to sew it together as you fasten off the end. If you like, embellish the flower with a wooden bead at the center.

MEDIUM COILED FLOWER *(Photo 2, page 25)*

Yarn: CYCA #1 (sock/fingering/baby) Mandarin Petit (100% cotton, 195 yd/178 m / 50 g; *see page 142*)

Crochet Hook: U.S. size D-3 / 3 mm

Ch 43.

Row 1: 1 dc in 4th ch from hook and then 1 dc in each st across; turn.

Row 2: Ch 2, 1 dc in 1st st, 1 dc in next st, (2 dc in next st, 1 dc in next st) across; turn.

Row 3: Change colors and then ch 2, 1 sc in 1st st, (ch 1, 1 sc in next st) across. Cut yarn, leaving a long tail and draw end through last st.

Coil the spiral into a flower shape (see photo) and use a few stitches to sew it together as you fasten off the end.

LARGE COILED FLOWER *(Photo 3, page 25)*

Yarn: CYCA #1 (sock/fingering/baby) Mandarin Petit (100% cotton, 195 yd/178 m / 50 g; *see page 142*)

Crochet Hook: U.S. size D-3 / 3 mm

Ch 33.

Row 1: Beginning in 2ⁿᵈ ch from hook, work 2 sc in each st across; turn = 64 sts.

Row 2: Ch 1, (1 sc in next st, 2 sc in next st) across; turn = 96 sts.

Row 3: Ch 1, (1 sc in each of next 2 sts, 2 sc in next st) across; turn = 128 sts.

Row 4: Ch 1, (1 sc in each of next 3 sts, 2 sc in next st) across; turn = 160 sts.

Row 5: Ch 1, (1 sc in each of next 4 sts, 2 sc in next st) across; turn = 192 sts.

Row 6: Ch 1, (1 sc in each of next 5 sts, 2 sc in next st) across; turn = 224 sts.

Cut yarn, leaving a long tail and draw end through last st.

Coil the spiral into a flower shape (see photo) and use a few stitches to sew it together as you fasten off the end. If you like, embellish the flower with a wooden bead at the center.

Butterflies

Who can resist a sweet little butterfly as a decoration? Add one to a headband, a hat, or embellish a child's sweater that needs some spiffing up. If you want a larger butterfly, use 2 strands of yarn held together and a larger crochet hook.

DECORATIVE BUTTERFLY

Yarn: CYCA #1 (sock/fingering/baby) Mandarin Petit (100% cotton, 195 yd/178 m / 50 g; *see page 142*)
Crochet Hook: U.S. size D-3 / 3 mm

Ch 4 and join into a ring with 1 sl st into 1st ch.
Rnd 1: (Ch 2, 3 dc around ring, ch 2, 1 sl st around ring) 2 times, (ch 1, 3 sc around ring, ch 1, 1 sl st around ring) 2 times. Cut yarn and draw end through last st.
Knot another color of yarn at the center of the butterfly's body and trim the yarn ends as antennas.

SMALL BUTTERFLY

Yarn: CYCA #1 (sock/fingering/baby) Mandarin Petit (100% cotton, 195 yd/178 m / 50 g; *see page 142*)
Crochet Hook: U.S. size D-3 / 3 mm

Ch 4 and join into a ring with 1 sl st into 1st ch.
Rnd 1: (Ch 3, 3 tr around ring, ch 3, 1 sl st around ring) 2 times, (ch 2, 3 dc around ring, ch 2, 1 sl st around ring) 2 times. Cut yarn and draw end through last st.
Knot another color of yarn at the center of the butterfly's body and trim the yarn ends as antennas.

Crochet the sweetest little hearts for decorating. Make a few to embellish a birthday present package or a hat, or to spruce up an already finished pillow. In the Christmas chapter of the book, the little heart is used for a garland (*see instructions on page 136*).

SMALL HEART

Yarn: CYCA #1 (sock/fingering/baby) Mandarin Petit (100% cotton, 195 yd/178 m / 50 g; *see page 142*)
Crochet Hook: U.S. size D-3 / 3 mm

Ch 4 and join into a ring with 1 sl st into 1st ch.
Rnd 1: All the sts are worked around the ring. Ch 2, 2 tr, 3 dc, ch 1, 1 tr, ch 1, 3 dc, 2 tr, ch 2; end with 1 sl st into 1st ch at beginning of rnd.
Rnd 2: Ch 2, 2 sc in each of next 2 tr, 1 sc in each of next 3 dc, ch 1, 3 sc in next tr, ch 1, 1 sc in each of next 3 dc, 2 sc in each of next 2 tr, ch 2, 1 sl st into sl st at end of Rnd 1. Cut yarn and draw end through last st. Weave in ends neatly on WS.

LARGE HEART

Yarn: CYCA #1 (sock/fingering/baby) Mandarin Petit (100% cotton, 195 yd/178 m / 50 g; see page 142)
Crochet Hook: U.S. size D-3 / 3 mm

Ch 6.
Row 1: 1 sc in 2nd ch from hook, 1 sc in each of the remaining 4 ch; turn.
Rows 2-4: Ch 1, 1 sc in each sc; turn.

Row 5: Ch 1, 1 sc in each sc; do not turn! Now you have crocheted a square; the rest of the heart is worked in the round.
Rnd 6: Working towards the left, work ch 3 (= 1 dc), 6 dc in the outermost sc at the center row of the side, 1 sl st into the last sc on Row 1, 7 dc in the center of the 5 sc on Row 1; skip 1 st, 1 sl st into next st.
Rnd 7: Ch 1, (1 sc in outermost sc of next row at side) 4 times, 2 sc in 1st sc of Row 5, 1 sc in each of the next 7 sts, 2 sc in each of the next 3 sts; 1 sc in next st, 1 sl st into next sl st, 1 sc in next st, 2 sc in each of the next 3 sts, 1 sc in each of the next 3 sts, 1 sl st in 1st sc; cut yarn and draw end through last st. Weave in ends neatly on WS.

For a Home

THE OPTIONS FOR CROCHETING INTERIOR DESIGN ITEMS FOR YOUR HOME are endless. I'll show you what I have in my home. You should consider this chapter as a source of inspiration because your needs and personal taste will vary. Start with what you already have at home and adjust the sizes accordingly.

Pillow with small granny squares

Yarn: CYCA #1 (sock/fingering/baby) Mandarin Petit (100% cotton, 195 yd/178 m / 50 g; *see page 142*)
Yarn Amounts: Leftover yarns in desired colors
Crochet Hook: U.S. size D-3 / 3 mm
Notions: Pillow form to fit into cover, approx. 2 in / 5 cm larger on each side than cover dimensions

Granny squares can be varied for all sorts of combinations to create different effects. You can play with different sizes and color combinations. This colorful pillow cover is large enough for a sofa pillow. It measures 15¾ x 15¾ in / 40 x 40 cm when finished and is composed of many small squares joined with a single color and measures when finished.

FRONT

You can find general instructions for a granny square on page 12. The front of the pillow cover is made with 6 x 6 squares (= 36 squares total) and each of the squares has a white center. For the second round of each square, I randomly chose orange, light pink, pink, cerise, turquoise, and light purple. For Round 3 (where I also joined the squares—*see page 14*), I used a darker purple for all of the squares. Large single-color pink squares frame the block of little squares in the cover. There are 8 large pink squares along each side. When all the squares have been joined and the ends neatly woven in on the wrong side, the front of the pillow cover is complete.

BACK

You can make the back of the cover different from the front. It is easiest to use fabric for the backing. You could also chain as many stitches as needed for the width of the cover and work back and forth in single crochet (sc), turning each row with ch 1 (= 1st sc) until the back is the same size as the front. The pillow shown here uses the same pink yarn as for the large squares framing the front and is worked as one very large granny square. Begin just as for a regular granny square and continue until it is the same dimensions as the front, 15¾ x 15¾ in / 40 x 40 cm. I worked 28 rounds for my large granny square before it was the right size.

FINISHING

If you crocheted a backing, finish the cover as follows: Place the front and back with RS of each facing out, just as the cover will be when finished. Crochet the pieces together. Insert the hook through both the front and back pieces and work sc around 3 sides of the cover. At each corner, work 3 sc into one stitch to round the corner. Insert the pillow form and then join the remaining side. It is little awkward to crochet with the pillow form inside but it usually goes well enough. For my pillow, I worked an additional round of sc. End the 2nd rnd with 1 sl st into the first st; cut yarn and draw end through last st. Weave the end to the inside and your pillow is finished! Here's an alternative for anyone who doesn't want to crochet a whole pillow.

Pillow with small flowers

This pillow cover is made with two plain white fabric squares decorated with colorful flowers. Who wouldn't be happy to have this in their bedroom?

Yarn: CYCA #1 (sock/fingering/baby) Mandarin Petit (100% cotton, 195 yd/178 m / 50 g; *see page 142*)
Yarn Amounts: Leftover yarns in desired colors
Crochet Hook: U.S. size D-3 / 3 mm
Notions: Plain white fabric, 2 squares approx. 19¾ x 19¾ in / 50 x 50 cm + seam allowances; matching sewing thread. Pillow form to fit into cover, approx. 2 in / 5 cm larger on each side than cover dimensions

FLOWER

Ch 4 and join into a ring with 1 sl st into 1st ch.
Rnd 1: Ch 4 (= 1st dc + ch 1), (1 dc around ring, ch 1) 5 times; end with ch 3 and 1 sl st into 3rd ch at beginning of rnd.

Rnd 2: Ch 1, 1 sc in 1st ch, (ch 3, 1 sc in next ch) 5 times; end with ch 3 and 1 sl st into 1st sc.
Rnd 3: Ch 1, around each ch loop, work (1 sc, ch 1, 3 dc, ch 1, 1 sc); end as for Rnd 2.
Cut yarn and draw end through last st. Weave in ends on WS.

FINISHING

A pillow cover 19¾ x 19¾ in / 50 x 50 cm could have 25 flowers (5 x 5). Sew the outer rows of flowers 2 in / 5 cm in from each side, about 4 in / 10 cm apart. Space remaining flowers to align with outer rows. Seam the cover on three sides, insert pillow form, and neatly seam fourth side.

Linnéa's pillow with wheel blocks

Yarn: CYCA #1 (sock/fingering/baby) Mandarin Petit (100% cotton, 195 yd/178 m / 50 g; *see page 142*) for all colors except Red
CYCA #3 (DK/light worsted) Marks & Kattens Flox (100% cotton, 153 yd/140 m / 50 g; *see page 142*)
Yarn Amounts: Approx. 100 g of Flox in Red 4747-1765; and leftovers of Mandarin Petit in Orange 2709, Pink 4505, Pink-Lilac 4915, Dark Lilac 5226, Light Turquoise 6803, Lime 8722, and Green 8514
Crochet Hook: U.S. size D-3 / 3 mm
Notions: Pillow form to fit into cover, approx. 2 in / 5 cm larger on each side than cover dimensions

SQUARE

Ch 4 and join into a ring with 1 sl st into 1st ch. End all rnds with 1 sl st into 2nd ch at beginning of rnd.

Rnd 1: Ch 2 (= 1st dc), 11 dc around ring = 12 dc.

Rnd 2: Ch 2, 1 dc in the space between dc of previous rnd and then 2 dc between every dc around = 12 dc groups.

Rnd 3: Sl st to 2nd dc, ch 2, 2 dc in space between dc group of previous rnd and then 3 dc in each space between dc groups = 12 dc groups.

Rnd 4: Sl st to 3rd dc, ch 1, (1 sc in space between dc groups, ch 4) around and end with 1 sl st into 1st sc.

Rnd 5: Ch 2, 2 dc around 1st ch loop, and then work 3 dc in each ch loop around but, work (3 dc, ch 1, 3 dc) in every 3rd ch loop for corner—make sure the piece has 4 corners

and is squared.

Rnd 6: Sl st to 3rd dc, ch 2, 2 dc in 1st space between dc groups, work 3 dc in each space between dc groups and (3 dc, ch 1, 3 dc) in each corner loop.

CROCHET SQUARES TOGETHER

When the 2nd square is almost done, crochet the first two squares together along one side as you work the last rnd, *following the instructions on page 14*. Make the next square and join squares as you work.

BACK

The pillow cover consists of 5 x 5 squares for a total of 25 squares. It measures 19¾ x 19¾ in / 50 x 50 cm. Chain a number of stitches to match the width of the front and work back and forth in single crochet (sc)—turn each row with ch 1 (=1st sc)—until the back is the same size as the front.

FINISHING

Place the front and back with RS of each facing out. Crochet the pieces together: insert the hook through both the front and back pieces and work sc around 3 sides of the cover. At each corner, work 3 sc into one stitch to round the corner. Insert the pillow form and then join the remaining side.

For my pillow, I worked an additional round: (1 sc, skip 2 sts, 5 dc, skip 2 sts) around. This makes a sawtooth edging. If you don't want a sawtooth edge, just work the final rnd with sc only.

Chevron pattern pillow

This pillow measures 15¾ x 23¾ in / 40 x 60 cm, but, of course, you can make it any size you like. Crochet as many chain stitches as you need for the width + a few more because the pattern makes the piece draw in. If you end up with too many stitches, you can easily hide the extra chain when you do the finishing. If you want to chain an exact number of stitches, chain a multiple of 12 + 2 stitches.

Yarn: CYCA #1 (sock/fingering/baby) Mandarin Petit (100% cotton, 195 yd/178 m / 50 g; *see page 142*)
Yarn Amounts: Approx. 200 g Pink 4505 and 100 g each of White 1001, Orange 2709, Red 4418, Cerise 4517, Light Turquoise 6803, Lime 8722, and Green 8514
Crochet Hook: U.S. size E-4 / 3.5 mm
Notions: Pillow form to fit into cover, approx. 2 in / 5 cm larger on each side than cover dimensions
NOTE: Hold yarn double throughout.

With two strands of yarn held together, loosely ch 134. The pattern begins and ends with a valley so it won't grow in the wrong direction—think of a V. The pattern begins with regular dc: 4 dc, 3 dc together, 4 dc, increase 3 dc, etc.

Row 1: Begin in the 3rd ch from hook (= 1st dc so only work 3 more dc before 1st valley) and work [4 dc, make a valley (see below), 4 dc, make a top, (see below)] across.

The stitch count should be sufficient that you can work a valley + 4 dc at the end of the row; turn.
Rows 2-58: Ch 2 (= 1st dc), 3 dc and then continue pattern with (valley, 4 dc, top, 4 dc) across; end with a valley + 4 dc. The valleys and tops should align on every row.

Top: Work 3 dc into 1 stitch.
Valley: Join 3 dc as follows: Yarn around hook, insert hook through stitch, yarn around hook, and bring yarn through st (= 3 loops on hook), yarn around hook and draw yarn through 2 loops on hook. Yarn around hook, insert hook into 2nd st, yarn around hook, and bring yarn through st (= 4 loops on hook), yarn around hook and through 2 loops on hook. Yarn around hook, insert hook into 3rd st, yarn around hook, and bring yarn through st (= 5 loops on hook), yarn around hook and through 2 loops on hook and then yarn around hook and through remaining 4 loops at the same time.
The pillow is worked in one piece. I changed colors after every row for a striped effect. Instead of waiting to weave in ends during finishing (there will be a lot of ends!), catch the ends as you work the first few stitches of a row.
My pillow has 58 rows for the size of cover I wanted. Since people crochet at different tensions, your pillow may be a different size.

FINISHING

When the pillow cover is large enough, fold it in half with the RS facing out. With edge to edge, crochet the cover together along one short side with sc. Insert the hook through stitches on both sides and draw the yarn through both stitches. At each corner, work 3 sc in the same stitch. Continue joining along the long side. Insert the pillow form and then join the other short side.

Chevron pattern pillow 2

This pillow measures 15¾ x 23¾ in / 40 x 60 cm, but, of course, you can make it any size you like. Crochet as many chain stitches as you need for the width + a few more because the pattern makes the piece draw in. If you end up with too many stitches, you can easily hide the extra chain when you do the finishing. If you want to chain an exact number of stitches, chain a multiple of 12 + 2 stitches.

Yarn: CYCA #1 (sock/fingering/baby) Mandarin Petit (100% cotton, 195 yd/178 m / 50 g; *see page 142*)
Yarn Amounts: Approx. 100 g each of Yellow 2315, Orange 2709, Turquoise 6705, Light Turquoise 6803, Green 8514, and Navy Blue 6073
Crochet Hook: U.S. size D-3 / 3 mm
Notions: Pillow form to fit into cover, approx. 2 in / 5 cm larger on each side than cover dimensions

Loosely ch 158. The pattern begins and ends with a valley so it won't grow in the wrong direction—think of a V. The pattern begins with regular dc: 4 dc, 3 dc together, 4 dc, increase to 3 dc, etc.

Row 1: Begin in the 3rd ch from hook (= 1st dc so only work 3 more dc before 1st valley) and work [4 dc, make a valley (see below), 4 dc, make a top, (see below)] across. The stitch count should be sufficient that you can work a valley + 4 dc at the end of the row; turn.

Rows 2-96: Ch 3 (= 1st dc), 3 dc and then continue pattern with (valley, 4 dc, top, 4 dc) across; end with a valley + 4 dc. The valleys and tops should align on every row.

Top: Work 3 dc into 1 stitch.
Valley: Join 3 dc as follows: Yarn around hook, insert hook through stitch, yarn around hook, and bring yarn through st (= 3 loops on hook), yarn around hook and draw yarn through 2 loops on hook. Yarn around hook, insert hook into 2nd st, yarn around hook, and bring yarn through st (= 4 loops on hook), yarn around hook and through 2 loops on hook. Yarn around hook, insert hook into 3rd st, yarn around hook, and bring yarn through st (= 5 loops on hook), yarn around hook and through 2 loops on hook and then yarn around hook and through remaining 4 loops at the same time.

The pillow is worked in one piece. I changed colors after every 4th row for a wide striped effect. Instead of waiting to weave in ends during finishing (there will be a lot of ends!), catch the ends as you work the first few stitches of a row.

My pillow has 96 rows for the size of cover I wanted. Since people crochet at different tensions, your pillow may be a different size.

FINISHING

When the pillow cover is large enough, fold it in half with the RS facing out. With edge to edge, crochet the

cover together along one short side with sc. Insert the hook through stitches on both sides and draw the yarn through both stitches. At each corner, work 3 sc in the

same stitch. Continue joining along the long side. Insert the pillow form and then join the other short side. Work another row along joining edge: (1 sc, 3 sc in next st, 1 sc).

Striped pillow

This is the easiest pillow cover imaginable so it's a good project for beginners. It's also a great match for a granny square blanket.

Yarn: CYCA #1 (sock/fingering/baby) Mandarin Petit (100% cotton, 195 yd/178 m / 50 g; *see page 142*)

Yarn Amounts: The example shown here used three colors—Light Turquoise 6803, Lime 8722, and Green 8514—with approx. 150 g of each color for a pillow measuring 23¾ x 11¾ in / 60 x 30 cm

Crochet Hook: U.S. size E-4 / 3.5 mm

Notions: Pillow form to fit into cover, approx. 2 in / 5 cm larger on each side than cover dimensions

NOTE: Hold yarn double throughout.

With two strands of yarn held together, ch 59.

Row 1: Begin in the 2nd ch from hook and work 1 sc in each ch across; turn.

Rows 2–110: Ch 1, work 1 sc in each st across; turn. In the pillow shown here, I changed colors on every 5th row.

Make two pieces alike. Place the pieces with RS facing out and join as follows. I used a different color than any I crocheted with for a nice finishing effect. Insert the hook through both layers (approx. 2 rows inside the edge and with 2 sts or 2 rows in between every st) and work sc around 3 sides of the cover, with 3 sc in each corner st. Insert pillow form and then join last side. For

one of my pillows, I added another rnd of sc. Cut yarn and draw end through last st. Weave in ends to WS.

Throw for the sofa

Yarn: CYCA #1 (sock/fingering/baby) Mandarin Petit (100% cotton, 195 yd/178 m / 50 g; *see page 142*) for all colors except Red
CYCA #3 (DK/light worsted) Marks & Kattens Flox (100% cotton, 153 yd/140 m / 50 g; *see page 142*)

Yarn Amounts: Just use whatever leftover yarns you have on hand. I used Flox in Red 4747-1765, and Mandarin Petit in White 1001, Yellow 2315, Orange 2709, Pink 4505, Light Pink 4301, Pink-Lilac 4915, Turquoise 6705, Medium Lilac 5314, Dark Lilac 5226, Light Turquoise 6803, Lime 8722, and Green 8514

Crochet Hook: U.S. size D-3 / 3 mm

The sofa throw is made with granny squares that are joined as you work *(see instructions on pages 12-15)*.

Each square is made with 7 rnds and the colors vary on each square. Most of the squares end with the 7th rnd worked in White, but, for greater effect, I finished some squares with Pink instead of White. The other rounds are worked with a variety of colors—see photos for color combination suggestions.

This throw is 9 squares wide and 14 squares long with a total of 126 squares that were crocheted together *(see page 14)*.
When all the squares have been crocheted and joined, and the ends woven in on the WS, make an edging all around. Begin in a ch space and work 3 dc in each space between dc groups on every square. At each corner, work as for the squares: (3 dc, ch 1, 3 dc).

Coverlet

To manage making a coverlet, I recommend that you crochet relatively simple squares that are rather large so you won't lose patience when only half the project is done and there are too many squares left to do.

Yarn: CYCA #1 (sock/fingering/baby) Mandarin Petit (100% cotton, 195 yd/178 m / 50 g; *see page 142*)

Yarn Amounts: For this coverlet, each skein of yarn will make 2 squares, so you'll need 84 skeins total of Natural White 1002, Yellow 2315, Orange 2709, Cerise 4517, Pink 4505, Light Pink 4301, Pink-Lilac 4915, Turquoise 6705, Light Turquoise 6803, Lime 8722, and Green 8514, plus approx. 6 skeins of White 1001 for joining.

Crochet Hook: U.S. size G-6 / 4 mm

NOTE: Hold yarn double throughout.

SQUARE

With two strands of yarn held together, ch 4 and join into a ring with 1 sl st into 1st ch. End every rnd with 1 sl st into the 3rd ch at beginning of round.

Rnd 1: Work all dc around ring. Ch 3 (= 1st dc), 2 dc, (ch 2, 3 dc) until there are 4 groups of dc total; end with ch 2 and join with 1 sl st into top of ch 3 at beginning of rnd.

Rnd 2: Ch 3, work 1 dc in each st around, with (2 dc, ch 2, 2 dc) in each corner.

Rnds 3-8: Work as for Rnd 2 with each round larger as you increase at each corner. After completing 8 rnds, cut yarn and draw end through last st. Weave in ends as you work.

This coverlet was designed for a double bed 71 in / 180 cm wide. For that size, you'll need 168 squares—which will form a rectangle 12 squares wide and 14 squares long. When all the squares have been worked, crochet them together. Place 2 squares edge to edge with the RS facing. With white yarn, work through both layers and sc along 1 side. Join squares into long strips and then join the strips across for the width. When all the squares have been joined, with white, work 1 rnd of sc around outer edge, with 3 sc in each corner st.

Ozzy's blanket

A colorful blanket big enough for a little boy's bed. This blanket, with 13 x 10 squares, measures approx. 47¼ x 35½ in / 120 x 90 cm when finished.

Yarn: CYCA #1 (sock/fingering/baby) Mandarin Petit (100% cotton, 195 yd/178 m / 50 g; *see page 142*)

Yarn Amounts: Just use whatever leftover yarns you have on hand. I used White 1001, Yellow 2315, Orange 2709, Red 4418, Pink 4505, Light Pink 4301, Turquoise 6705, Light Lilac 5212, Light Turquoise 6803, Lime 8722, and Green 8514

Crochet Hook: U.S. size D-3 / 3 mm

To make the granny squares, see instructions on page 12. All the squares have the same colors at the center (yellow and orange) but different colors on the following 3 rounds. They were all finished and joined with turquoise. Each square has a total of 6 rounds. When all the squares are complete, lay them out in the order they will be joined. Work 1 sc in the side of a square, ch 1, then 1 sc on the side of the second square that the first is joined to. Ch 1 again, skip 1 st on the first square and work 1 sc more on the first square. Continue crocheting the squares together the same way. I didn't add an outer edging so that I can add more squares as my son grows.

In Swedish, there are two kinds of granny squares. Squares that are worked completely with double crochet and without the lace effect of "mother's mother" granny squares are called "father's mother" granny squares. This little blanket is large enough for a newborn. Every other square is white and the others are a variety of colors. Each square measures approximately 3¾ x 3¾ in / 9.5 x 9.5 cm and the blanket is 30 x 22½ in / 76 x 57 cm.

Yarn: CYCA #1 (sock/fingering/baby) Mandarin Petit (100% cotton, 195 yd/178 m / 50 g; *see page 142*)
Yarn Amounts: If you crochet tightly, you should get 4-5 squares out of each skein of yarn. I used White 1001, Cerise 4517, Pink 4505, Turquoise 6705, Light Turquoise 6803, Lime 8722, and Green 8514
Crochet Hook: U.S. size D-3 / 3 mm

SQUARE

Ch 4 and join into a ring with 1 sl st into 1st ch. End all rnds with 1 sl st into 3rd ch at beginning of rnd.

Rnd 1: Work all dc around ring. Ch 1 (=1st dc), 2 dc, repeat (ch 1, 3 dc) until there are 4 groups of dc total; end with ch 1.

Rnd 2: Ch 3, work 1 dc in each st around, with (2 dc, ch 1, 2 dc) in each corner st.

Rnds 3-6: Work as for Rnd 2 with each round larger as you increase at each corner. After completing 6 rnds, cut yarn and draw end through last st. Weave in ends as you work.

Leo's blanket

Yarn: CYCA #1 (sock/fingering/baby) Mandarin Petit (100% cotton, 195 yd/178 m / 50 g; *see page 142*) for all colors except Red
CYCA #3 (DK/light worsted) Marks & Kattens Flox (100% cotton, 153 yd/140 m / 50 g; *see page 142*)
Yarn Amounts: 300 g of Flox in Red 4747-1765; Mandarin Petit: 100 g Turquoise 6705, 200 g White 1001, and 150 g each of Light Turquoise 6803, Green 8514, and Navy Blue 6073
Crochet Hook: U.S. size D-3 / 3 mm

SQUARE

Leo's blanket is made with granny squares (*see page 12*) that are joined as you work (see page 14). Each square consists of 2 rnds Turquoise in the center and then 4 rnds of a single color. Every other square uses White for the outer rounds. The last round is crocheted with Red as the squares are joined. This blanket is 12 squares wide and 15 squares long for a total of 180 squares.

After all the squares have been crocheted and joined, crochet an edging. Begin with Red and 1 sc in each st around, with 3 sc in each corner st. Change to Navy Blue and work in dc all around (begin rnd with ch 3 as the 1st dc), with 3 dc in each corner st. Finish with another round in sc with Turquoise, increasing at corners as before.

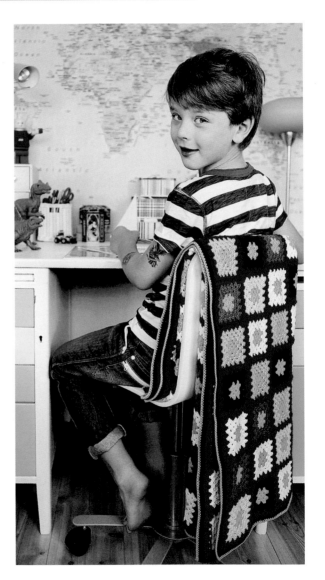

Granny square potholder

Yarn: CYCA #1 (sock/fingering/baby) Mandarin Petit (100% cotton, 195 yd/178 m / 50 g; *see page 142*) or similar size leftover yarn
Crochet Hook: U.S. size C-2 / 2.5 mm

SQUARE

Ch 4 and join into a ring with 1 sl st into 1st ch. End every rnd with 1 sl st into 3rd ch at beginning of rnd. Cut yarn at end of each rnd and change colors.

Rnd 1: Work all dc around ring. Ch 3 (= 1st dc), 1 dc, (ch 1, 2 dc) around until there are 8 dc groups; end with ch 1.
Rnd 2: Work all dc around the ch-1 loop between dc groups of previous rnd. Ch 3, 2 dc, (ch 1, 3 dc) around; end with ch 1.
Rnd 3: Ch 3, 2 dc, and then alternate: (ch 1, 3 dc) and (ch 1, 3 dc, ch 1, 3 dc) in the loops between dc groups so that you end up with 4 corners. On the last rnd, crochet the squares together (*see instructions on page 14*).
Each potholder consists of 9 squares that are crocheted together. This potholder has two layers so make a block of 9 squares for each side. Join the layers with the RS facing out and work an edging *at the same time*:
Rnd 1: When working the sc, insert the hook through both layers so that they are crocheted together. Work (1 sc, ch 3, skip 3 sts) around.
Rnd 2: Work 5 sc in each ch loop around.
Rnd 3: (1 sc, skip 2 sts, 5 dc in next st, skip 2 sts) around. Finish with ch 15-20 for the hanging loop; attach with 1 sl st into potholder so the ch forms a loop. Work sc around the loop, filling it well. Cut yarn and draw end through last st. Weave in all ends to inside.

Square potholder 1

Yarn: CYCA #1 (sock/fingering/baby) Mandarin Petit (100% cotton, 195 yd/178 m / 50 g; *see page 142*) or similar size leftover yarn
Crochet Hook: U.S. size C-2 / 2.5 mm

Ch 4 and join into a ring with 1 sl st into 1st ch. End every rnd with 1 sl st into 3rd ch at beginning of rnd.

Rnd 1: Work all dc around ring. Ch 3 (= 1st dc), 2 dc, (ch 1, 3 dc) around until you have 4 dc groups; end with ch 1.

Rnd 2: Ch 3, work 1 dc in each st around, with (2 dc, ch 1, 2 dc) in each corner st.

Rnds 3-11: Work as for Rnd 2, with each round larger as you increase at each corner. Change colors as you like. For example, I changed colors after Rnd 2.

After completing 11 rnds, cut yarn and draw end through last st. Weave in ends as you work.

The potholder is doubled so make 2 layers the same way. Join the layers with the RS facing out and work an edging *at the same time*:

Rnd 1: When working the sc, insert the hook through both layers so that they are crocheted together. Work (1 sc, ch 3, skip 2 sts) around all four sides.

Rnd 2: Work 3 sc in each ch-3 loop around.

Rnd 3: (1 sc, skip 2 sts, 5 dc in next st, skip 2 sts) around. Finish with ch 15-20 for the hanging loop; attach with 1 sl st into potholder so the ch forms a loop. Work sc around the loop, filling it well. Cut yarn and draw end through last st. Weave in all ends to inside.

Yarn: CYCA #1 (sock/fingering/baby) Mandarin Petit (100% cotton, 195 yd/178 m / 50 g; *see page 142*) or similar size leftover yarn

Crochet Hook: U.S. size C-2 / 2.5 mm

Begin by following the instructions for the granny square on page 12. Work 7 rnds. For my potholder, I changed colors after Rnds 1, 4, and 7.

Rnds 8-10: Ch 3 (= 1st dc), work 1 dc in each st around, with (2 dc, ch 1, 2 dc) in each corner st; end rnd with 1 sl st into top of ch 3 at beginning of rnd.

Cut yarn and draw end through last st of Rnd 10. Weave in all ends neatly on WS. The potholder is doubled so make 2 layers the same way. Join the layers with the RS facing out and work an edging at the same time:

Rnd 1: When working the sc, insert the hook through both layers so that they are crocheted together. Work (1 sc, ch 3, skip 2 sts) around all four sides.

Rnd 2: Work 3 sc in each ch-3 loop around.

Finish with ch 15-20 for the hanging loop; attach with 1 sl st into potholder so the ch forms a loop. Work sc around the loop, filling it well. Cut yarn and draw end through last st. Weave in all ends to inside.

Round potholder

Yarn: CYCA #1 (sock/fingering/baby) Mandarin Petit (100% cotton, 195 yd/178 m / 50 g; *see page 142*) or similar size leftover yarn

Crochet Hook: U.S. size C-2 / 2.5 mm

Ch 4 and join into a ring with 1 sl st into 1st ch. End every rnd with 1 sl st into 3rd ch at beginning of rnd.

Rnd 1: Ch 3 (= 1st dc), work 11 dc around ring = 12 dc.

Rnd 2: Ch 3, 1 dc into sl st at beginning of rnd and then 2 dc in each st around = 24 dc.

Rnd 3: Ch 3, 2 dc in next st, work (1 dc in next st, 2 dc in next st) around.

Rnd 4: Ch 3, 1 dc in next st, 2 dc in next st, work (1 dc in each of next 2 sts, 2 dc in next st) around.

Rnd 5: Ch 3, 1 dc in each of next 2 sts, 2 dc in next st, work (1 dc in each of next 3 sts, 2 dc in next st) around.

Rnd 6: Ch 3, 1 dc in each of next 3 sts, 2 dc in next st, work (1 dc in each of next 4 sts, 2 dc in next st) around.

Rnd 7: Ch 3, 1 dc in each of next 4 sts, 2 dc in next st, work (1 dc in each of next 5 sts, 2 dc in next st) around.

Rnd 8: Ch 3, 1 dc in each of next 5 sts, 2 dc in next st, work (1 dc in each of next 6 sts, 2 dc in next st) around.

Rnd 9: Ch 3, 1 dc in each of next 6 sts, 2 dc in next st, work (1 dc in each of next 7 sts, 2 dc in next st) around.

Cut yarn and draw end through last st of Rnd 9. Weave in all ends neatly on WS. The potholder is doubled so make 2 layers the same way. Join the layers with the RS facing out and work an edging *at the same time:*

Rnd 1: When working the sc, insert the hook through both layers so that they are crocheted together. Work (1 sc between 2 dc, ch 3, skip 3 sts) around.

Rnd 2: Work 3 sc in each ch-3 loop around.

Rnd 3: Work (1 sc, skip 2 sts, 5 dc in next st, skip 2 sts) around.

Finish with ch 15-20 for the hanging loop; attach with 1 sl st into potholder so the ch forms a loop. Work sc around the loop, filling it well. Cut yarn and draw end through last st. Weave in all ends to inside.

Old-fashioned potholder

This pattern comes from an old potholder that I found at a flea market. Maybe one of your grandmothers made one just like it?

Yarn: CYCA #1 (sock/fingering/baby) Mandarin Petit (100% cotton, 195 yd/178 m / 50 g; *see page 142*) or similar size leftover yarn
Crochet Hook: U.S. size D-3 / 3 mm

Ch 5 and join into a ring with 1 sl st into 1st ch. End every rnd with 1 sl st into 3rd ch at beginning of rnd.
Rnd 1: Ch 3 (= 1st dc), work 19 dc around ring = 20 dc.
Rnd 2: Ch 3, 1 dc, ch 2, (2 dc, ch 2) around. Change colors.

Note: On Rnds 3-6, work all dc around ch loop of previous rnd.
Rnd 3: Sl st to next ch loop, (ch 3, 1 dc, ch 1, 2 dc) in first ch loop; work (2 dc, ch 1, 2 dc) in each ch loop around.
Rnd 4: Sl st to next ch loop, (ch 3, 2 dc, ch 2, 3 dc) in first ch loop; work (3 dc, ch 2, 3 dc) in each ch loop around.
Rnd 5: Sl st to next ch loop, (ch 3, 3 dc, ch 3, 4 dc) in first ch loop; work (4 dc, ch 3, 4 dc) in each ch loop around.
Rnd 6: Sl st to next ch loop, (ch 3, 4 dc, ch 4, 5 dc) in first ch loop; work (5 dc, ch 4, 5 dc) in each ch loop around. Change colors.
Rnd 7: Work 1 sc in the space between dc groups, ch 2, (13 dc around next ch loop, ch 2, 1 sc in space between dc groups, ch 2) around, ending with 1 sl st into 1st sc. Change colors.
Rnd 8: Begin at a dc group and work (1 dc in each of next 3 sts, 2 dc in each of next 7 sts, 1 dc in each of next 3 sts) around. Change colors.
Rnd 9: Work 1 sc in each st around.
Finish with ch 15-20 for the hanging loop; attach with 1 sl st into potholder so the ch forms a loop. Work sc around the loop, filling it well. Cut yarn and draw end through last st. Weave in all ends to inside.

Apple holder

A practical little holder for an apple so it isn't damaged on the way to your job or to school. It's a very simple project, so why not make each family member one in a different color?

Yarn: CYCA #1 (sock/fingering/baby) Mandarin Petit (100% cotton, 195 yd/178 m / 50 g; *see page 142*) or similar size leftover yarn
Crochet Hook: U.S. size E-4 / 3.5 mm
Notions: 1 button to fit button loop; matching sewing thread
NOTE: Hold yarn double throughout.

With two strands of yarn held together, ch 4 and join into a ring with 1 sl st into 1st ch. End every rnd with 1 sl st into the 1st sc at beginning of rnd.
Rnd 1: Ch 1, work 6 sc around ring = 6 sts.
Rnd 2: Ch 1, work 2 sc in each sc around = 12 sts.
Rnd 3: Ch 1, work (1 sc in next st, 2 sc in next st) around = 18 sts.
Rnd 4: Ch 1, work (1 sc in each of next 2 sts, 2 sc in next st) around = 24 sts.
Rnd 5: Ch 1, work (1 sc in each of next 3 sts, 2 sc in next st) around = 30 sts.
Rnd 6: Ch 1, work 1 sc in each st around = 30 sts.
Rnd 7: Ch 1, work (1 sc in each of next 4 sts, 2 sc in next st) around = 36 sts.
Rnd 8: Ch 1, work 1 sc in each st around = 36 sts.

Rnd 9: Ch 1, work (1 sc in each of next 5 sts, 2 sc in next st) around = 42 sts.
Rnd 10: Ch 1, work 1 sc in each st around = 42 sts
After completing Rnd 10, turn at the end of each row to create a slit that will be closed with a button.
Rows 11-15: Ch 1, and then work 1 sc in each st across. On Row 11, work until 1 st remains and turn.
Row 16: Ch 2, alternately working through front loop of 1 st and then back loop of next, work 1 dc in each st across.
Ch 10 and finish with 1 sl st to attach the loop; cut yarn and draw end through last st. Weave in ends on WS. Sew on a button to fit loop.

Mug cozy

Mug cozies are very decorative and, most of all, it is so comforting to hold a warm cup. The cozy is easy to make and will fit most mugs. The design can easily be adjusted for the circumference of the cup and made shorter or longer to fit your mug. Fit your own mug now!

Yarn: CYCA #1 (sock/fingering/baby) Mandarin Petit (100% cotton, 195 yd/178 m / 50 g; *see page 142*) or similar size leftover yarn
Crochet Hook: U.S. size E-4 / 3.5 mm
Notions: 2 buttons to fit through double crochet row, matching sewing thread
NOTE: Hold yarn double throughout.

With two strands of yarn held together, ch 17.
Row 1: Beginning in 2nd ch from hook, work 1 sc in each ch across; end with ch 1; turn.
Rows 2–41: Work 1 sc in each st across, working into back loops only; end row with ch 1; turn.
Row 42: Ch 3 and then work 1 dc in each st across; end with ch 1; turn. The row of dc creates the buttonholes.
Row 43: Work in sc across; cut yarn and draw end through last st. Weave in ends on WS. Sew on two buttons.

Coasters

Small and oh-so-sweet flowery coasters for your table. The small one is suitable for glasses and coffee cups and the large one for tea mugs.

SMALL COASTER

Yarn: CYCA #1 (sock/fingering/baby) Mandarin Petit (100% cotton, 195 yd/178 m / 50 g; *see page 142*) or similar size leftover yarn
Crochet Hook: U.S. size E-4 / 3.5 mm
NOTE: Hold yarn double throughout.

With two strands of yarn held together, ch 4 and join into a ring with 1 sl st into 1st ch.
Rnd 1: Ch 3 (= 1st dc), work 15 dc around ring = 16 dc; end with 1 sl st into top of ch 3 at beginning of rnd.
Rnd 2: Ch 3, 1 dc in sl st, 2 dc in each of rem sts = 32 dc; end with 1 sl st into top of ch 3 at beginning of rnd.
Rnd 3: Ch 1, 1 sc in sl st, 1 sc in each of next 2 st, 2 sc in next st, (1 sc in each of next 3 st, 2 sc in next st) around = 40 sc; end with 1 sl st into 1st sc.
Rnd 4: Ch 1, 1 sc in each of next 5 sts, ch 3, (1 sc in each of next 5 sts, ch 3) around; end with 1 sl st into 1st sc.
Rnd 5: Sl st to 3rd sc, ch 1, (1 sc in 3rd sc, 7 dc around ch-3 loop) around; end with 1 sl st into 1st sc. Cut yarn and weave in ends on WS.

LARGE COASTER

Yarn: CYCA #1 (sock/fingering/baby) Mandarin Petit (100% cotton, 195 yd/178 m / 50 g; *see page 142*) or similar size leftover yarn
Crochet Hook: U.S. size E-4 / 3.5 mm
NOTE: Hold yarn double throughout.

With two strands of yarn held together, ch 4 and join into a ring with 1 sl st into 1st ch.
Rnd 1: Ch 3 (= 1st dc), work 15 dc around ring = 16 dc; end with 1 sl st into top of ch 3 at beginning of rnd.
Rnd 2: Ch 3, 1 dc in sl st, 2 dc in each of rem sts = 32 dc; end with 1 sl st into top of ch 3 at beginning of rnd.
Rnd 3: Ch 3, 2 dc in next st, (1 dc, 2 dc in next st) around = 48 dc; end with 1 sl st into top of ch 3 at beginning of rnd.
Rnd 4: Ch 3, 1 dc, 2 dc in next st, (1 dc in each of next 2 sts, 2 dc in next st) around = 64 dc; end with 1 sl st to top of ch 3 at beginning of rnd.
Rnd 5: Ch 1, 1 sc in sl st, 1 sc in each of next 6 sts, 2 sc in next st, (1 sc in each of next 7 st, 2 sc in next st) around = 72 sc; end with 1 sl st into 1st sc ch 3, (5 sc, ch 3) around; end with.
Rnd 6: Ch 1, 1 sc in each of next 6 sts, ch 3, (1 sc in each of next 6 sts, ch 3) around; end with 1 sl st into 1st sc.
Rnd 7: Sl st to 3rd sc, ch 1, (1 sc in 3rd sc, 7 dc around ch-3 loop) around; end with 1 sl st into 1st sc. Cut yarn and weave in ends on WS.

Coat hanger covers

You can usually find old-style wooden hangers for a good price at flea markets. You don't need a lot of skill to crochet a hanger cover so this is a good project for beginners. With many bright colors, these hangers are so pretty you won't want to hide them away in the closet!

STRIPED HANGER COVER

Yarn: CYCA #1 (sock/fingering/baby) Mandarin Petit (100% cotton, 195 yd/178 m / 50 g; *see page 142*) or leftover yarn of a similar weight
Crochet Hook: U.S. size D-3 / 3 mm

Ch 16.
Row 1: Beginning in 2nd ch from hook, work 1 sc in each ch across; turn.
Rows 2-88: Ch 1, 1 sc in each st across; turn.
The number of rows needed depends on how loosely or tightly you crochet and how big your hangers are. When the piece is long enough, cut the yarn and draw end through last st.
Fold the piece down the length and crochet it together. Begin at one short end. In the examples shown here, the joining yarn is a different color than those used for the rest of the project. Work single crochet (sc) through both layers, spacing the sts evenly. When the short end has been joined, join the long side. Before joining the other short side, insert the hanger: unscrew the hook, slide the hanger in and then join the short end; screw the hook back in.

The hangers shown in the photos are decorated with crocheted flowers and hearts. See the chapter "A Little Extra for Decoration" for additional inspiration.

SPOTTED HANGER COVER

The covers for these hangers were crocheted in two separate pieces and then crocheted together.

Yarn: CYCA #1 (sock/fingering/baby) Mandarin Petit (100% cotton, 195 yd/178 m / 50 g; *see page 142*) or similar size leftover yarn
Crochet Hook: U.S. size D-3 / 3 mm

Ch 98.
Row 1: In 2nd ch from hook, work 1 sc, (skip 2 ch, 5 dc in next ch, skip 2 ch, 1 sc) across.
Row 2: Turn piece upside down and work on opposite side of foundation chain. Work as for Row 1, making sure that the dc groups align.
Row 3: Change colors and work around the "spots", with 3 sc above each spot and (1 hdc, ch 1, 1 hdc) between each spot.
Set piece aside and make another the same way (Rows 1-3).
Row 4: When both side of the hanger are complete, join with single crochet. Beginning at one long side, sc across, down short side, and then other long side. Unscrew the hook from the hanger and insert the hanger into the cover; join short end. Cut yarn and draw end through last st. Screw hook back into hanger.

Fish mobile

Here's a cute little mobile of multi-color fish. Make it whatever length works for your home.

Yarn: CYCA #1 (sock/fingering/baby) Mandarin Petit (100% cotton, 195 yd/178 m / 50 g; *see page 142*)
Yarn Amounts: Each fish only uses a small amount of yarn, so leftover yarns work well
Crochet Hook: U.S. size D-3 / 3 mm
Notions: Eyes for the fish. I used toy safety eyes available in craft stores (embroider on eyes instead of using safety eyes if mobile will be handled by children under age 3). Fiberfill for the fish. Beads for decoration—I used brightly colored wooden beads and a little bell for the end. Elastic cord to string the fish and beads onto.

BODY

Ch 4 and join into a ring with 1 sl st into 1st ch. End all rnds with 1 sl st into 1st ch to complete the round.
Rnd 1: Ch 1, 6 sc around ring = 6 sts.
Rnd 2: Ch 1, (1 sc in next st, 2 sc in next st) around = 9 sts.
Rnd 3: Ch 1, (1 sc in each of next 2 sts, 2 sc in next st) around = 12 sts.
Rnd 4: Ch 1, (1 sc in each of next 3 sts, 2 sc in next st) around = 15 sts.
Rnd 5: Ch 1, (1 sc in each of next 4 sts, 2 sc in next st) around = 18 sts.
Rnd 6: Ch 1, 1 sc in each st around = 18 sts.
Rnd 7: Ch 1, (1 sc in each of next 5 sts, 2 sc in next st) around = 21 sts.

Rnds 8–10: Ch 1, 1 sc in each st around = 21 sts.
Set in the eyes. Use safety eyes with a post and backing.
Rnd 11: Ch 1, (1 sc in each of next 5 sts, decrease over next 2 sts = insert hook into next st, yarn around and through st; insert hook into next st, yarn around and through st = 3 loops on hook; yarn around and through all 3 loops at once) 2 times; end with 1 sc in each of next 3 sts, decrease as above 2 times = 17 sts rem.
Rnd 12: Ch 1, (1 sc in each of next 4 sts, decrease) 2 times, end with 1 sc in each of next 3 sts, decrease = 14 sts rem.
Rnd 13: Ch 1, (decrease) 7 times = 7 sts rem.

FIN

Rnd 14: Ch 1, (2 sc in next st) 7 times = 14 sts.
Rnd 15: Ch 1, (2 sc in next st) 7 times = 28 sts.
Rnd 16: Ch 1, 1 sc in each st around = 28 sts.
Rnd 17: Ch 1, 1 sc in each st around = 28 sts.
Rnd 18: Pinch the fin together and join the layers with sc. Cut yarn and draw end through last st. Weave in ends to WS.

Make as many fish as you like. I made 7 for my mobile. If you want larger fish, work with 2 strands of yarn held together and hook U.S. size E-4 / 3.5 mm.
Thread the fish and beads onto the elastic cord, knotting ends well to secure.

Crocheted pennants

Pennants are very popular for decorating children's rooms these days. Why not make a crocheted version in bright colors? You can decide on how long or short to make them.

Yarn: CYCA #1 (sock/fingering/baby) Mandarin Petit (100% cotton, 195 yd/178 m / 50 g; *see page 142*)
Yarn Amounts: You can get 4-5 pennants from each skein of yarn. I used Orange 2709, Red 4418, Pink 4505, and Light Turquoise 6803
Crochet Hook: U.S. size D-3 / 3 mm

Ch 26.
Row 1: 1 sc in 2nd ch from hook, 1 sc in each of next 24 ch, ch 1; turn.
Row 2: 1 sc in each of next 25 sts, ch 1; turn.
Continue back and forth in sc, decreasing at beginning and end of every 4th row: 1 sl st into 1st sc, ch 1, 1 sc in 2nd sc, sc across until 1 st remains; turn = 2 sts decreased. When 3 sts remain, cut yarn and draw end through last st. Edge the piece with sc along both sides (but not the top). Weave in ends neatly on WS.
Join the pennants: Ch 50, (sc across top of pennant, ch 20) until 1 pennant remains, sc across last pennant and then ch 50. Cut yarn and draw end through last st.
TIP: To help the pennants lie flat, spray them with water and then lightly steam press them.

Why not dress up an old stool with a crocheted cover made from brightly colored granny squares? Of course, stools vary in size and shape, but the pattern is designed as an example to inspire you.

Yarn: CYCA #1 (sock/fingering/baby) Mandarin Petit (100% cotton, 195 yd/178 m / 50 g; *see page 142*) CYCA #3 (DK/light worsted) Marks & Kattens Flox (100% cotton, 153 yd/140 m / 50 g; *see page 142*)
Yarn Colors: Flox in Red 4747-1765; Mandarin Petit in White 1001, Orange 2709, Pink 4505, Medium Lilac 5314, Light Turquoise 6803, and Green 8514
Crochet Hook: U.S. size D-3 / 3 mm

The cover is made with granny squares (*see page 12*) joined together as you work (*see page 14*). Each square has 4 rnds and the same color sequence for the first 3 rnds. The colors for the 4th rnd vary. The seat on my stool measures 12¾ x 12¾ in / 32 x 32 cm. For that size, I worked 5 x 5 squares with a total of 25 squares. When all the squares have been crocheted and joined, work an edging. Insert the hook into a space between dc groups and bring yarn through, work 3 dc in each space around, with only 1 dc group at each corner (instead of the usual 3 dc, ch 1, 3 dc). The "short" corners draw in the cover to shape it around the stool. I crocheted 7 rounds for my cover edging.

Spring Fresh and Summer Fine

FINALLY SPRING AND SUMMER ARE HERE AGAIN after the long, dark winter. With milder temperatures and the lovely spring light, I feel an unbelievably strong longing for bright, pretty colors. This is the perfect time to revel in fine crocheted accessories and garments.

Triangular shawl of flowers

A fresh shawl in dainty, spring-like colors crocheted following the same method as the flowery scarf in the fall and winter chapter (*see page 104*). These flowers are arranged in a triangle rather than around as for the scarf.

Yarn: CYCA #1 (sock/fingering/baby) Mandarin Petit (100% cotton, 195 yd/178 m / 50 g; *see page 142*)

Yarn Amounts: Yarn needed depends on the size you want. The example shown here used 7 colors: White 1001, Natural White 1002, Orange 2709, Light Pink 4301, Pink 4505, Pink-Lilac 4915, and Light Turquoise 6803

Crochet Hook: U.S. size D-3 / 3 mm

FLOWER

Ch 8 and join into a ring with 1 sl st into 1st ch.

Rnd 1: Ch 3, 1 dc, (ch 2, 2 dc around ring) 11 times, ch 2, 1 sl st into top of ch 3 at beginning of rnd = 12 dc groups).

Rnd 2: Sl st to the 1st ch loop, ch 1, 1 sc in ch loop, (ch 9, 1 sc in same ch loop, ch 5, 1 sc in next ch loop, ch 5, 1 sc in next ch loop) around. End with 1 sl st into 1st ch = 6 large and 12 small ch loops.

Rnd 3: Sl st to the next ch-9 loop, ch 4 (= 1st tr), 8 tr, ch 3, 9 tr around same ch-9 loop, [1 sc in next ch loop, 1 sc in next ch loop, (9 tr, ch 3, 9 tr) in same ch-9 loop] around. End with 1 sl st into top of ch 4 at beginning of rnd. When you are at the tip of each flower petal, join the flowers with 1 sc. Lay the flower petals next to each other and work 1 sc through the second petal before you continue to finish the petal you began with.
In the example here, I began with one flower, the next row has 2 flowers, the third row has 3 flowers, etc. Continue until you have 11 flowers across the top row.

Simple hat with a flower

Hats are fun and just the right size of project. A hat requires accurate counting to make sure the stitch count is correct, but otherwise it's easy. Place a contrast color yarn marker at the beginning of the round so you can keep track of where you are.

This easy and wonderful hat can be varied in so many ways. Make a single-color version with a brightly-colored flower or a fresh-looking striped hat. You can decide if you want a baggy or close-fitting hat.

Yarn: CYCA #1 (sock/fingering/baby) Mandarin Petit (100% cotton, 195 yd/178 m / 50 g; *see page 142*)

Yarn Amounts: Approx. 100 g for the hat and leftover yarns for the flower, in desired colors

Crochet Hook: U.S. size E-4 / 3.5 mm

NOTE: Hold yarn double throughout.

With two strands of yarn held together, ch 4 and join into a ring with 1 sl st in 1st ch. End every rnd with 1 sl st into 1st st to complete the rnd.

Rnd 1: Ch 1, 6 sc around ring = 6 sts.

Rnd 2: Ch 1, 2 sc in each st around = 12 sts.

Rnd 3: Ch 1, (1 sc in next st, 2 sc in next st) around = 18 sts.

Rnd 4: Ch 1, (1 sc in each of next 2 sts, 2 sc in next st) around = 24 sts.

Rnd 5: Ch 1, (1 sc in each of next 3 sts, 2 sc in next st) around = 30 sts.

Rnd 6: Ch 1, (1 sc in each of next 4 sts, 2 sc in next st) around = 36 sts.

Rnd 7: Ch 1, (1 sc in each of next 5 sts, 2 sc in next st) around = 42 sts.

Rnd 8: Ch 1, 1 sc in each st around = 42 sts.

Rnd 9: Ch 1, (1 sc in each of next 6 sts, 2 sc in next st) around = 48 sts.

Rnd 10: Ch 1, 1 sc in each st around = 48 sts.

Rnd 11: Ch 1, (1 sc in each of next 7 sts, 2 sc in next st) around = 54 sts.

Rnd 12: Ch 1, 1 sc in each st around = 54 sts.

Rnd 13: Ch 1, (1 sc in each of next 8 sts, 2 sc in next st) around = 60 sts.

Rnd 14: Ch 1, 1 sc in each st around = 60 sts.

Rnd 15: Ch 1, (1 sc in each of next 9 sts, 2 sc in next st) around = 66 sts.

Rnd 16: Ch 1, 1 sc in each st around = 66 sts.

Rnd 17: Ch 1, (1 sc in each of next 10 sts, 2 sc in next st) around = 72 sts.

Rnd 18: Ch 1, 1 sc in each st around = 72 sts.

Rnd 19: Ch 1, (1 sc in each of next 11 sts, 2 sc in next st) around = 78 sts.

Rnd 20: Ch 1, 1 sc in each st around = 78 sts.

Rnd 21: Ch 1, (1 sc in each of next 12 sts, 2 sc in next st) around = 84 sts.

For large child's size, stop increasing here.

Rnd 22 (adult size only): Ch 1, 1 sc in each st around = 84 sts.

Rnd 23 (adult size only): Ch 1, (1 sc in each of next 13 sts, 2 sc in next st) around = 90 sts.

For adult size, stop increasing here.

For all sizes, continue as follows:

Ch 1, work 1 sc in each st around. Repeat this round until hat is the length you want, approx. 8¼ in / 21 cm for a regular sizing and approx. 9¾ in / 25 cm for a looser hat. Change to a new color for the last two rounds so the edging on the hat will be distinctive. The length measurements above do not include the 2-round edging.

The examples shown in these photos are decorated with flowers sewn on (*see instructions for "Flower in several*

layers with a 'wheel' at the center" on page 18). You can also add a round of slip stitch on the RS of the hat above the last two edging rounds (as for hat shown on page 70).

Fine spotted tam

Isn't this tam pretty with all its spots? Of course, it's a little extra work to crochet all the spots and sew them onto the tam, but well worth the effort by the time you are finished. This pattern is for a little one but it's easy to adapt for larger sizes.

Yarn: CYCA #1 (sock/fingering/baby) Mandarin Petit (100% cotton, 195 yd/178 m / 50 g; *see page 142*)

Yarn Amount: Approx. 100 g for the tam and leftover yarns for the spots, in desired colors

Crochet Hook: U.S. size D-3 / 3 mm

Ch 4 and join into a ring with 1 sl st in 1st ch. End every rnd with 1 sl st into 1st ch to complete the rnd.

Rnd 1: Ch 1, 6 sc around ring.

Rnd 2: Ch 1, 2 sc in each st around = 12 sc.

Rnd 3: Ch 1, (1 sc in next st, 2 sc in next st) around = 18 sts.

Rnd 4: Ch 1, (1 sc in each of next 2 sts, 2 sc in next st) around = 24 sts.

Rnd 5: Ch 1, (1 sc in each of next 3 sts, 2 sc in next st) around = 30 sts.

Rnd 6: Ch 1, (1 sc in each of next 4 sts, 2 sc in next st) around = 36 sts.

Rnd 7: Ch 1, (1 sc in each of next 5 sts, 2 sc in next st) around = 42 sts.

Rnd 8: Ch 1, (1 sc in each of next 6 sts, 2 sc in next st) around = 48 sts.

Rnd 9: Ch 1, (1 sc in each of next 7 sts, 2 sc in next st) around = 54 sts.

Rnd 10: Ch 1, (1 sc in each of next 8 sts, 2 sc in next st) around = 60 sts.

Rnd 11: Ch 1, (1 sc in each of next 9 sts, 2 sc in next st) around = 66 sts.

Rnd 12: Ch 1, (1 sc in each of next 10 sts, 2 sc in next st) around = 72 sts.

Rnd 13: Ch 1, (1 sc in each of next 11 sts, 2 sc in next st) around = 78 sts.

Rnd 14: Ch 1, (1 sc in each of next 12 sts, 2 sc in next st) around = 84 sts.

Rnd 15: Ch 1, (1 sc in each of next 13 sts, 2 sc in next st) around = 90 sts.

Rnd 16: Ch 1, (1 sc in each of next 14 sts, 2 sc in next st) around = 96 sts.

Rnd 17: Ch 1, (1 sc in each of next 15 sts, 2 sc in next st) around = 102 sts.

Rnd 18: Ch 1, (1 sc in each of next 16 sts, 2 sc in next st) around = 108 sts.

Rnd 19: Ch 1, (1 sc in each of next 17 sts, 2 sc in next st) around = 114 sts.

Rnd 20: Ch 1, (1 sc in each of next 18 sts, 2 sc in next st) around = 120 sts.

Rnd 21: Ch 1, (1 sc in each of next 19 sts, 2 sc in next st) around = 126 sts.

Rnd 22: Ch 1, (1 sc in each of next 20 sts, 2 sc in next st) around = 132 sts.

Rnd 23: Ch 1, (1 sc in each of next 21 sts, 2 sc in next st) around = 138 sts.

Rnd 24: Ch 1, 1 sc in each st around (138 sts).
Repeat Rnd 24 until hat measures approx. 8 in / 20 cm long.

When hat is desired length, shape crown as follows:

Rnd 1: Ch 1, [21 sc, sc2tog (insert hook into next st, yarn around hook and through st, hook through next st, yarn around hook and through st = 3 loops on hook; yarn around hook and through all 3 loops at once)] around = 132 sts rem.

Rnd 2: Ch 1, (20 sc, sc2tog) = 126 sts rem.

Rnd 3: Ch 1, (19 sc, sc2tog) = 120 sts rem.

Rnd 4: Ch 1, (18 sc, sc2tog) = 114 sts rem.

Rnd 5: Ch 1, (17 sc, sc2tog) = 108 sts rem.

Rnd 6: Ch 1, (16 sc, sc2tog) = 102 sts rem.

Rnd 7: Ch 1, (15 sc, sc2tog) = 96 sts rem.

At this point, you can start adjusting the size. The example shown here is for a smaller child. If you want a larger size, you can make the hat longer before you begin decreasing but you may not need to decrease on as many rows as above.

End with working 2 rounds sc in a contrast color to make a pretty edging.

The hat in the photo is decorated with crocheted spots that are sewn on (see below for instructions). We also worked 1 round slip stitch on the RS of the hat, *above* the 2 final contrast color rounds. After fastening off all the ends, you can tie a bow with the yarn tails instead of trimming them.

SPOTS

Ch 4 and join into a ring with 1 sl st in 1st ch.

Rnd 1: Ch 1, 6 sc around ring.

Rnd 2: Ch 1, 2 sc in each st around = 12 sc.

Cut yarn, leaving a tail long enough for sewing on spot, and draw end through last st.

For this hat, we used approx. 40 spots in 6 different colors.

Summer hat

A wonderful summer hat in pretty colors protects against the sun's strong rays. Make a lovely, single-color hat or a brightly striped one. It will look good on both big and small.

Yarn: CYCA #1 (sock/fingering/baby) Mandarin Petit (100% cotton, 195 yd/178 m / 50 g; *see page 142*)
Yarn Amount: Approx. 100 g for all sizes, in desired colors
Crochet Hook: U.S. size C-2 / 2.5 mm for a tighter fabric

Ch 4 and join into a ring with 1 sl st in 1st ch. End every rnd with 1 sl st into 1st ch to complete the rnd.

Rnd 1: Ch 1, 6 sc around ring = 6 sts.
Rnd 2: Ch 1, 2 sc in each st around = 12 sts.
Rnd 3: Ch 1, (1 sc in next st, 2 sc in next st) around = 18 sts.
Rnd 4: Ch 1, (1 sc in each of next 2 sts, 2 sc in next st) around = 24 sts.
Rnd 5: Ch 1, (1 sc in each of next 3 sts, 2 sc in next st) around = 30 sts.
Rnd 6: Ch 1, (1 sc in each of next 4 sts, 2 sc in next st) around = 36 sts.
Rnd 7: Ch 1, (1 sc in each of next 5 sts, 2 sc in next st) around = 42 sts.
Rnd 8: Ch 1, (1 sc in each of next 6 sts, 2 sc in next st) around = 48 sts.
Rnd 9: Ch 1, (1 sc in each of next 7 sts, 2 sc in next st) around = 54 sts.
Rnd 10: Ch 1, (1 sc in each of next 8 sts, 2 sc in next st) around = 60 sts.
Rnd 11: Ch 1, (1 sc in each of next 9 sts, 2 sc in next st) around = 66 sts.
Rnd 12: Ch 1, (1 sc in each of next 10 sts, 2 sc in next st) around = 72 sts.
Rnd 13: Ch 1, 1 sc in each st around = 72 sts.
Rnd 14: Ch 1, (1 sc in each of next 11 sts, 2 sc in next st) around = 78 sts.
Rnd 15: Ch 1, 1 sc in each st around = 78 sts.
Rnd 16: Ch 1, (1 sc in each of next 12 sts, 2 sc in next st) around = 84 sts.
Rnd 17: Ch 1, 1 sc in each st around = 84 sts.
Rnd 18: Ch 1, (1 sc in each of next 13 sts, 2 sc in next st) around = 90 sts.
Rnd 19: Ch 1, 1 sc in each st around = 90 sts.
Rnd 20: Ch 1, (1 sc in each of next 14 sts, 2 sc in next st) around = 96 sts.
Rnd 21: Ch 1, 1 sc in each st around = 96 sts.
Rnd 22: Ch 1, (1 sc in each of next 15 sts, 2 sc in next st) around = 102 sts.
Rnd 23: Ch 1, 1 sc in each st around = 102 sts.
Rnd 24: Ch 1, (1 sc in each of next 16 sts, 2 sc in next st) around = 108 sts.

End increases for small child's size here and work around in sc without increasing until hat is approx. 6¼ in / 16 cm long.

Next rnd: Ch 3, work 1 dc in each st around and end with 1 sl st into top of ch 3 = 108 dc. Go to Rnd 1 of the brim below.

Large child's and adult sizes continue:

Rnd 25: Ch 1, 1 sc in each st around = 108 sts.

Rnd 26: Ch 1, (1 sc in each of next 17 sts, 2 sc in next st) around = 114 sts.

End increases for large child's size here and work around in sc without increasing until hat is approx. 6¾ in / 17 cm long.

Next rnd: Ch 3, work 1 dc in each st around and end with 1 sl st into top of ch 3 = 114 dc. Go to Rnd 2 of the brim below.

Adult size continues:

Rnd 27: Ch 1, 1 sc in each st around = 114 sts.

Rnd 28: Ch 1, (1 sc in each of next 18 sts, 2 sc in next st) around = 120 sts.

Rnd 29: Ch 1, 1 sc in each st around = 120 sts.

Repeat Rnd 29 until hat is approx. 7½ in / 19 cm long.

Next rnd: Ch 3, work 1 dc in each st around and end with 1 sl st into top of ch 3 = 120 dc. Go to Rnd 3 of the brim below.

BRIM

Rnd 1: Ch 1, (1 sc in each of next 17 sts, 2 sc in next st) around = 114 sts.

Rnd 2: Ch 1, (1 sc in each of next 18 sts, 2 sc in next st) around = 120 sts.

Rnd 3: Ch 1, (1 sc in each of next 19 sts, 2 sc in next st) around = 126 sts.

Rnd 4: Ch 1, (1 sc in each of next 20 sts, 2 sc in next st) around = 132 sts.

Rnd 5: Ch 1, (1 sc in each of next 21 sts, 2 sc in next st) around = 138 sts.

Rnd 6: Ch 1, (1 sc in each of next 22 sts, 2 sc in next st) around = 144 sts.

Rnd 7: Ch 1, (1 sc in each of next 23 sts, 2 sc in next st) around = 150 sts.

Rnd 8: Ch 1, (1 sc in each of next 24 sts, 2 sc in next st) around = 156 sts.

Rnd 9: Ch 1, (1 sc in each of next 25 sts, 2 sc in next st) around = 162 sts.

Rnd 10: Ch 1, (1 sc in each of next 26 sts, 2 sc in next st) around = 168 sts.

Rnd 11: Ch 1, (1 sc in each of next 27 sts, 2 sc in next st) around = 174 sts.

Rnd 12: Ch 1, (1 sc in each of next 28 sts, 2 sc in next st) around = 180 sts.

Rnd 13: Ch 1, (1 sc in each of next 29 sts, 2 sc in next st) around = 186 sts.

Rnd 14: Ch 1, (1 sc in each of next 30 sts, 2 sc in next st) around = 192 sts.

Rnd 15: Ch 1, (1 sc in each of next 31 sts, 2 sc in next st) around = 198 sts.

Rnd 16: Ch 1, 1 sc in each st around = 198 sts.

Rnd 17: Ch 1, (1 sc in each of next 32 sts, 2 sc in next st) around = 204 sts.

Rnd 18: Ch 1, 1 sc in each st around = 204 sts.
End increases for small child's hat here and finish by working Rnds 22-24 (204) sts.

Large child's and adult size hats only:

Rnd 19: Ch 1, (1 sc in each of next 33 sts, 2 sc in next st) around = 210 sts.

Rnd 20: Ch 1, 1 sc in each st around = 210 sts.
End increases for large child's hat here and finish with Rnds 22-24 (210) sts.

Adult size hat only:

Rnd 21: Ch 1, (1 sc in each of next 34 sts, 2 sc in next st) around = 216 sts.

Rnds 22-24 (all sizes): Ch 1, 1 sc in each st around = 216 sts.

The hat shown in the photo above was embellished with a "Large Coiled Flower" (*see instructions on page 25*).

Wrist warmers with butterflies

Wrist warmers are easy to crochet and, worked in pretty colors, are nice accessories for kids—or why not make a pair for yourself before the sun warms up too much? The wrist warmers shown here are sized for a three-year-old, but it's easy to make a larger size if you want. For a larger circumference and length, add extra chain stitches at the beginning for a longer cuff and add extra rows in both the ribbing and the overall length.

Yarn: CYCA #1 (sock/fingering/baby) Mandarin Petit (100% cotton, 195 yd/178 m / 50 g; *see page 142*)
Yarn Amount: Approx. 50 g Light Turquoise 6803 and leftover yarns for the details (I used Pink 4505)
Crochet Hook: U.S. size D-3 / 3 mm

With cuff color, ch 6.
Row 1: Work 1 sc in 2nd ch from hook and then 1 sc in each ch across; turn.
Rows 2-29: Ch 1, 1 sc in each of next 5 sts, working into back loops only; turn.
After completing ribbing, fold with RS facing RS and seam short ends: crochet together with sc through both layers. Change yarn color and turn ribbing, so you can pick up stitches along one long side.
Rnd 1: Work 33 sc evenly spaced across the ribbed cuff, ending with 1 sl st into 1st sc.
First Pattern Rnd: Ch 2, 2 dc in same space as chain, (skip 2 sts, 3 dc in next st) around; end with 1 sl st into top of ch 2 at beginning of rnd.

All Following Pattern Rnds: Ch 2, work 3 dc in each space between dc groups; end with 1 sl st into top of ch 2. Work a total of 12 pattern rounds.
Rnd 13: Increase by 1 dc group: in 1st space between dc groups, work (3 dc, ch 1, 3 dc). Continue rnd as set. Work another 9 pattern rnds without increasing.
End with 2 rnds of sc in contrast color; cut yarn and draw end through last st. Weave in all ends on WS. The wrist warmers in the photo above are decorated with a "Small butterfly" (*see instructions on page 26*).

Rainbow-striped leg warmers

The leg warmers shown here are sized for a one-year old but you can easily adjust the size. Just add more chain stitches for the ribbing and add more rows to the ribbing and leg length to make the leg warmers wider and longer.

Yarn: CYCA #1 (sock/fingering/baby) Mandarin Petit (100% cotton, 195 yd/178 m / 50 g; *see page 142*)

Yarn Colors: Pink 4505, Red 4418, Orange 2709, Yellow 2315, Green 8514, Pink-Lilac 4915, and Turquoise 6705

Yarn Amounts: Depends on size; the pair shown here used approx. 100 g total of leftover yarns

Crochet Hook: U.S. size D-3 / 3 mm

Ch 9.

Row 1: Work 1 sc in 2nd ch from hook and then 1 sc in each ch across; turn.

Rows 2-36: Ch 1, 1 sc in each of next 8 sts, working into back loops only; turn.

After completing ribbing, fold with RS facing RS and seam short ends: crochet together with sc through both layers.

Turn ribbing so you can pick up stitches along one long side.

Rnd 1: Work 37 sc evenly spaced across the ribbed cuff, ending with 1 sl st into 1st sc.

Rnd 2: Change colors, ch 1, work 1 sc in each st around; end with 1 sl st into first sc.

Continue around in sc, changing colors every 7th rnd. Our

example used pink for the ribbing and 1st rnd and then 7 rnds each of Red, Orange, Yellow, Green, Pink-Lilac, and Turquoise. End with 2 rnds sc in pink. Cut yarn and draw end through last st. Weave in all ends on WS.

Necklace

A pretty, colorful necklace will dress up any outfit. Use a variety of yarn colors or mix in wooden beads, which you can buy at a craft store.

Yarn: CYCA #1 (sock/fingering/baby) Mandarin Petit (100% cotton, 195 yd/178 m / 50 g; *see page 142*)
Yarn Amounts: Leftover yarns in desired colors
Crochet Hook: U.S. size C-2 / 2.5 mm
Notions: fiberfill, elastic cord, wooden beads

CROCHETED NECKLACE BEADS

Ch 4 and join into a ring with 1 sl st into the 1st ch. End all rnds with 1 sl st into 1st ch to complete round.

Rnd 1: Ch 1, 6 sc around ring = 6 sts.

Rnd 2: Ch 1, work 2 sc in each st around = 12 sts.

Rnd 3: Ch 1, work (1 sc in next st, 2 sc in next st) around = 18 sts.

Rnds 4–6: Ch 1, 1 sc in each st around = 18 sts.

Rnd 7: Ch 1, [1 sc in next st, sc2tog (insert hook into next st, yarn around hook and through st, hook through next st, yarn around hook and through st = 3 loops on hook; yarn around hook and through all 3 loops at once)] around = 12 sts rem. Before continuing, stuff the bead with fiberfill.

Rnd 8: Ch 1, sc2tog around = 6 sts rem.

Rnd 9: Ch 1, sc2tog around = 3 sts rem.

Cut yarn, leaving tail long enough to close bead and weave in; draw end through last st. String beads onto elastic cord, knotting at bead ends to secure them. Make sure necklace is securely joined.

For the necklace shown here, I decided not to string beads all around so that the necklace wouldn't be too bulky—this necklace has 10 crocheted beads.

Bracelet with small granny squares

Bracelets are fun, easy to make, and unbelievably decorative. This bracelet consists of one- or two-round granny squares joined together. It's an easy little project that you can make in an evening.

I used a small size crochet hook for the bracelet so it would be as firm as possible but still flexible enough.

Yarn: CYCA #1 (sock/fingering/baby) Mandarin Petit (100% cotton, 195 yd/178 m / 50 g; *see page 142*)
Crochet Hook: U.S. size B-1 / 2 mm
Notions: Button to fit button loop, matching sewing thread

See page 12 for "Granny squares." As shown in photos, you can work 1- or 2-round squares.

Ch 4 and join into a ring with 1 sl st into 1st ch.
Rnd 1: Ch 3, 2 dc around ring, (ch 1, 3 dc around ring) 3 times; end with ch 1 and 1 sl st into top of ch 3 = 4 dc groups. Cut yarn and draw end through last st.
After completing the first square, begin the second one, joining the squares at each corner. On last rnd of square, work 3 dc at corner and then join with 1 sc in the corner of the first square. Continue around to the corner of 2nd square. Join the second corner as for the first so that the two squares are joined in two of the corners.
When bracelet is as long as you want (adult size is about 10 squares), work sc all around for an edging. Begin and end at the short ends. Finish with ch 10 and secure it to

band with 1 sl st into same space as beginning of chain. Sew on a button at the opposite end. Lightly steam press the bracelet on WS to iron out any bunching.

Bracelet with large granny squares

Yarn: CYCA #1 (sock/fingering/baby) Mandarin Petit (100% cotton, 195 yd/178 m / 50 g; *see page 142*)
Crochet Hook: U.S. size B-1 / 2 mm
Notions: Button to fit button loop, matching sewing thread

Ch 4 and join into a ring with 1 sl st into 1st ch.
Rnd 1: Ch 3, 2 dc around ring, (ch 1, 3 dc around ring) 3 times; end with ch 1 and 1 sl st into top of ch 3 = 4 dc groups. Cut yarn and draw end through last st if changing colors.
Rnd 2: Insert hook under last worked ch loop and bring yarn through, ch 3, 2 sc, ch 1, 3 dc around ch loop, [skip 3 dc and work (3 dc, ch 1, 3 dc) around next ch loop] around, ending with skip 3 dc, 1 sl st into top of ch 3 at beginning of rnd = 8 3-dc groups. Cut yarn and draw end through last st.
After completing the first square, begin the second one, joining the squares at each corner on Rnd 2. Work 3 dc at corner and then join with 1 sc in the corner of the first square. Continue around to the corner of 2nd square. Join the second corner as for the first so that the two squares are joined in two of the corners.
When bracelet is as long as you want (adult size is about 7 squares), work sc all around for an edging. Begin and end at the short ends. Finish with ch 10 and secure it to band with 1 sl st into same space as beginning of chain. Sew on a button at the opposite end. Lightly steam press the bracelet on WS to iron out any bunching.

Crocheted child's dress

This wonderful little crocheted dress is right out of the 1970s. When I was little, I had one almost exactly like it. This pattern was designed by my mother from her memory of it. Thank you, Mom!

Size: 12/18 months
Finished Measurements
Chest: Approx. 20 in / 51 cm
Total Length: Approx. 14¼ in / 36 cm
Yarn: CYCA #1 (sock/fingering/baby) Mandarin Petit (100% cotton, 195 yd/178 m / 50 g; *see page 142*)
Yarn Amounts: 150 g Light Pink 4301 and 50 g Pink 4505
Crochet Hook: U.S. size D-3 / 3 mm
Gauge: 24 dc and 13 rows = 4 x 4 in / 10 x 10 cm

BACK YOKE

Holding two strands of Light Pink together, ch 63. Cut one strand and turn. Beginning in 2nd ch from hook, sc across = 62 sc. Work a total of 4 rows in sc, turning with ch 1 on each row.

Armhole shaping: at each side, sl st over at beginning of row and skip sts at end of row: 3-1-1-1-1 sts. Next, decrease on every other row 1-1-1 sts = 42 sts rem. When back measures 2¾ in / 7 cm, divide piece at center for back placket and work each side separately = 21 sts on each side. Work back and forth in sc until piece is 4¾ in / 12 cm long.

Shape neck: On each of the next 3 rows, decrease 3-3-3 sts at neck edge = 12 sts rem.

Work opposite side of neck the same way.

FRONT YOKE

Work as for back yoke, including armhole shaping but omitting placket, until front is 3½ in / 9 cm long.

Shape neck: Leave the center 12 sts unworked for the neck and work each side separately. Work 15 sc; turn. Continue back and forth in sc, and, over the next 5 rows, decrease 2-1-1-1-1 sts at neck edge. When front yoke is 4¾ in / 12 cm long,

Shape shoulder: Over the next 3 rows, decrease 3-3-3 sts at neck edge. Work opposite side of yoke the same way.

SKIRT

With Light Pink, ch 120 and join into a ring with 1 sl st into 1st ch. Work 1 rnd with 1 sc in each st, working through back loops only. The front loops will be used later for joining the rings between the skirt and yoke.

Now begin pattern: Ch 2 (= 1st dc), 1 dc in each of the next 6 sts, [skip 2 sts, (3 dc, ch 1, 3 dc) in next st, skip 2 sts, 1 dc in each of next 7 sts] 9 times. End rnd with skip 2 sts, (3 dc, ch 1, 3 dc) in next st, skip 2 sts, 1 sl st into top of ch 2 at beginning of rnd. On the following rnds, work (3 dc, ch 1, 3 dc) around ch loop of previous round's dc group. Increase 2 dc on the 3rd pattern rnd by working 2 dc in the 2nd and 6th st of each solid dc part of the row = 9 dc. Continue increasing 2 dc on every 5th rnd 3 times. Set skirt aside until the rings are complete.

RINGS

With Pink, ch 10 and join into a ring with 1 sl st into 1st ch. Work 32 sc around ring and, *at the same time*, join to a stitch (join a ring on every 8th st) from the front/back yokes and the skirt.

FINISHING

Seam the yokes and, before completing skirt length, crochet the rings between the skirt and yoke. Continue skirt as set until the dress, including the rings, is 14¼ in / 36 cm long.

EDGINGS AND PLACKET

Beginning at the back placket, with Pink and RS facing, loosely work in sl st up towards the neck and around. Make sure the edging is flexible. Turn with ch 1 and then work around in sc through both stitch loops. Next row = picot edging: Ch 1 (skip 1 sc, 1 sl st, ch 3, 1 sl into same sc) around, ending with skip 1 sc, 1 sc in the last sc. Cut yarn and draw end through last st. Work the same edging around the armholes and then work 1 rnd sc around lower edge of skirt. If desired, add ch 10 at back of neck to final row of edging for button loop and sew on button.

Long cardigan

This cardigan also reminds me of the 1970s. Because it's a little lacy, it is especially nice over a fine little summer dress.

Size: 6 months (1, 2, 3) years

Finished Measurements

Chest: 21¾ (22½, 23¼, 24) in / 55 (57, 59, 61) cm

Sleeve Length: 8 (9½, 11, 12¾) in / 20 (24, 28, 32) cm

Total Length (down center back): Approx. 17 (18½, 20½, 23¾) in / 43 (47, 52, 60) cm

Yarn: CYCA #1 (sock/fingering/baby) Mandarin Petit (100% cotton, 195 yd/178 m / 50 g; *see page 142*)

Yarn Amounts: 150 (150, 200, 200) g

Crochet Hook: U.S. size D-3 / 3 mm

Notions: 5 (6, 6, 7) buttons, matching sewing thread

Gauge: 20 dc and 20 sts in pattern = 4 in / 10 cm; 11 rows = 4 in / 10 cm

Pattern—*see chart on page 84*

Increase 1 dc = work 2 dc in the same st

Decrease 1 dc = Yarn around hook, insert hook into next st, yarn around hook and through st = 3 loops on hook; yarn around hook and through 2 loops. Yarn around hook, insert hook into next st, yarn around hook and through st = 4 loops around hook. Yarn around hook and through 2 loops. Yarn around hook and through rem 3 loops on hook.

"Binding off" = at the beginning of a row, sl st over the number of sts specified; at the end of the row omit the number of sts specified; turn.

CARDIGAN SKIRT

Ch 145 (155, 165, 175).

Row 1: Skip 3 ch (= 1st dc), work 3 (2, 1, 0) dc, [15 sts Pattern 1, 10 (12, 14, 16) dc, 5 sts Pattern 2, 10 (12, 14, 16) dc] 3 times, 15 sts Pattern 1, 4 (3, 2, 1) dc.

Row 2: On Row 2 and all following rows, begin with ch 3 = 1st dc, skip 1 dc and, at end of row, work last dc in the top of ch 3. Continue as set up on Row 1.

Rows 3 and following: Decrease 1 dc at each side of pattern 2: work until 3 sts rem to pattern 2, decrease 1 dc, work 1 dc, 5 sts pattern 2, 1 dc, decrease 1 dc.

Repeat the decreases on every 6th row 6 (6, 5, 7) times, work 3 rows, decrease as before on every 4th row 0 (1, 3, 2) times until 107 (111, 115, 119) sts rem.

NOTE: When Pattern 1 is complete, repeat the last 6 rows until the piece is finished. When the whole piece measures 12¾ (13¾, 15½, 18¼) in / 32 (35, 39, 46) cm, cut yarn and draw end through last st. Weave in ends on WS.

BACK YOKE

Crochet in pattern over the center 47 (49, 53, 55) sts as before. On the 2nd row, begin shaping armholes at each side: on every row, omit 3-1-1-1 (2-1-1; 2-1-1; 2-1) sts until 37 (41, 45, 49) sts rem. When yoke measures 3½ (4, 4¼, 4¾) in / 9 (10, 11, 12) cm, shape shoulders on every row: at each side, omit 4-3-3 (4-4-3; 5-4-4; 5-5-4) sts. *At the same time as first shoulder decrease*, omit the center 17 (19, 19, 21) sts for

PATTERN 1

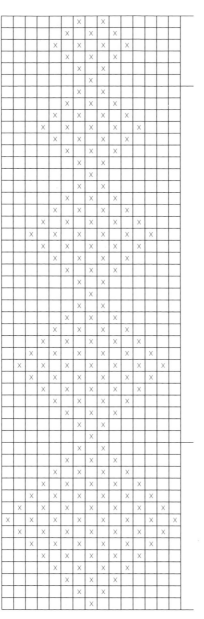

X

Repeat X to X

X

PATTERN 2

$\boxed{X}$ = ch 1, skip 1 st

$\square$ = 1 dc in dc or 1 dc around ch 1 loop

Begin size 6 months (1 year) here

Begin size 2 (3) years here

dc and then, at the end of the row, work the last dc over top of ch 3. Otherwise, work Row 2 as for Row 1.

Row 3 and all following rows: Increase 1 dc at each side inside the outermost edge st on every 3rd row until there are 42 (44, 48, 50) sts. When sleeve is 5¼ (6¾, 8, 9½) in / 13 (17, 20, 24) cm long, shape sleeve hat at each side by omitting 4-3-1 (4-3; 4-3; 4-3) sts at each side and then omit 2 sts at each side until sleeve hat is 2½ (2½, 2¾, 2¾) in / 6 (6, 7, 7) cm long. Cut yarn and draw end through last st. Weave in all ends on WS.

LOWER EDGE

Beginning on RS, work 3 rows sc; on the 1st row, work 1 sc in each dc and ch st. Cut yarn and draw end through last st. Weave in ends on WS.

FINISHING

Block the pieces by placing them, patted out to finished measurements, between damp towels. Leave until completely dry. Seam the garment. With RS facing, work in sc around the front edges and neck for 3 rows: on the 1st row, work 2 sc in each row and 2 sc in each st; on all 3 rows, work 3 sc at each corner. On the 2nd row, make 5 (6, 6, 7) buttonholes on the right front edge: Place the top one directly under the corner at the neck edge, with the rest spaced evenly below so that the last one is approx. 4¼ (5¼, 6, 6¾ in / 11 (13, 15, 17) cm from the lower edge. Make each buttonhole as follows: ch 2, skip 2 sts. On the next row, work 2 sc around each ch-2 buttonhole loop.

Lightly steam press the seams. Sew on the buttons. Make a cord with the yarn and thread through the last row at top of skirt; tie into a bow at front edge.

back neck. Work each side separately to complete shoulders.

FRONT YOKE

Skip 10 (8, 8, 6) sts at each side of back, work pattern crochet for each side of the front 22 (23, 25, 26) sts as before. Shape armhole as for back. When front yoke measures 2½ (2½, 2¾, 3¼) in / 6 (6, 7, 8) cm, omit 5-2 (6-2; 6-2; 7-2) sts at neck edge. When front yoke measures 3½ (4, 4¼, 4¾) in / 9 (10, 11, 12) cm, shape shoulder as for back.

SLEEVES (MAKE BOTH ALIKE)

Ch 34 (36, 36, 38).
Row 1: Skip 3 ch (= 1st dc), work 2 (3, 3, 4) dc, [5 sts Pattern 2, 2 dc] 3 times, 5 sts pattern 2, 3 (4, 4, 5) dc.
Row 2: On Row 2 and all following rows, ch 3 = 1st dc, skip 1

Granny square vest

If you like granny squares as much as I do, what can be cuter than a granny square vest to go with those fine summer outfits? You can make this vest for children and adults.

Size: 2-4 (6-8, 10-12 years; women's sizes 6-8, 10-12, 14-16)

Finished Measurements

Chest: 21¾ (26, 30¼, 32½, 36¾, 41) in / 55 (66, 77, 82.5, 93.5, 104.5) cm + edgings

Total Length (as measured down center back):
Approx. 10¾ (13, 13, 15¼, 17¼, 17¼) in / 27.5 (33, 33, 38.5, 44, 44) cm

Yarn: CYCA #1 (sock/fingering/baby) Mandarin Petit (100% cotton, 195 yd/178 m / 50 g; *see page 142*)

Yarn Amounts:
Main color (MC): 100 (100, 100, 150, 200, 200) g
Contrast Color 1 (CC1): 50 (50, 50, 50, 50, 100) g
Contrast Color 2 (CC2): 50 (50, 50, 50, 50, 100) g

Crochet Hook: U.S. size D-3 / 3 mm

Gauge: 1 square = 2¼ x 2¼ in / 5.5 x 5.5 cm

SQUARE 1

With CC1, ch 6 and join into a ring with 1 sl st into 1st ch.

Rnd 1: Ch 3 (= 1st dc), 2 dc around ring, (ch 2, 3 dc around ring) 3 times, ch 2; end with 1 sl st into top of ch 3 at beginning of rnd = 4 dc groups. Cut yarn and draw end through last st.

Rnd 2: With CC2, insert hook into last-worked ch loop and bring yarn through, ch 3, 2 dc, ch 2, 3 dc around same loop, [skip 3 dc, (3 dc, ch 2, 3 dc) around next ch loop] 3 times; skip 3 dc; end with 1 sl st into top of ch 3 at beginning of rnd = 8 dc groups. Cut yarn and draw end through last st.

Rnd 3: With MC, skip 1st group of ch 3 + 2 dc of previous rnd, insert hook around the corner ch loop, bring yarn through, (ch 3, 2 dc, ch 2, 3 dc) around same ch loop, [skip 3 dc and work 3 dc in next space between dc groups, skip 3 dc and work (3 dc, ch 2, 3 dc) around corner loop] 3 times and end with skip 3 dc 3 dc in next space between dc groups, skip 3 dc and join with 1 sl st into top of ch 3 at beginning of rnd (= 12 3-dc groups). Cut yarn and draw end through last st.

JOINING SQUARES

Crochet the total number of whole and half squares as indicated on the schematic for your size *on page 88*. Crochet the squares together in strips and then, with WS facing, crochet strips together with sc. Insert hook in the spaces between dc. Begin and end around corner sts. Join the two half squares as shown in photo to shape neck.

HALF SQUARES (MAKE 2 TO SHAPE NECKLINE)

With CC1, ch 6 and join into a ring with 1 sl st into 1st ch.

Rnd 1: Ch 3 (= 1st dc), 3 dc around ring, ch 2, 4 dc around ring. Cut yarn and draw end through last st.

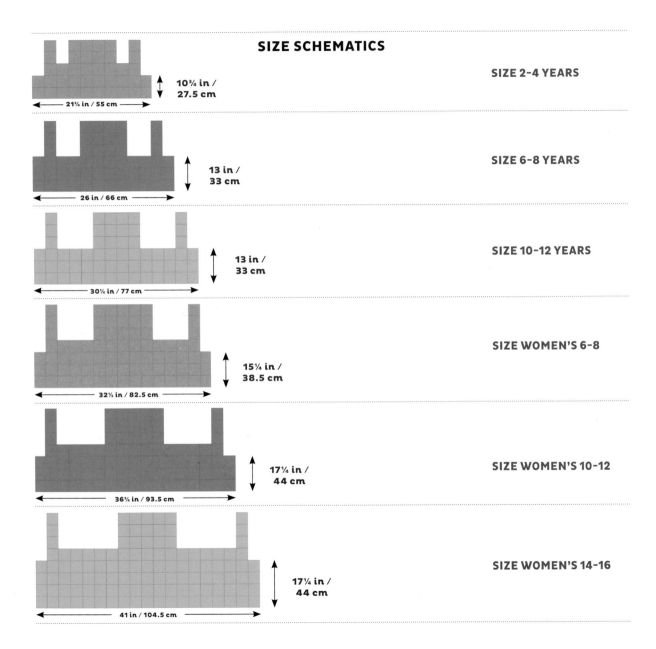

SIZE SCHEMATICS

SIZE 2-4 YEARS

10¾ in / 27.5 cm

21¾ in / 55 cm

SIZE 6-8 YEARS

13 in / 33 cm

26 in / 66 cm

SIZE 10-12 YEARS

13 in / 33 cm

30¼ in / 77 cm

SIZE WOMEN'S 6-8

15¼ in / 38.5 cm

32½ in / 82.5 cm

SIZE WOMEN'S 10-12

17¼ in / 44 cm

36¾ in / 93.5 cm

SIZE WOMEN'S 14-16

17¼ in / 44 cm

41 in / 104.5 cm

Rnd 2: With CC2, insert hook between the ch-3 and first dc of previous round and bring yarn through. Ch 3, 3 dc in same space, skip 3 dc, (3 dc, ch 2, 3 dc) around the ch-2 loop, skip 3 dc, 4 dc between the 3rd and 4th dc. Cut yarn and draw end through last st.

Rnd 3: With MC, insert hook in the space between the ch-3 and first dc of previous rnd and bring yarn through, ch 3, 3 dc in same space, skip 3 dc, 3 dc in next space, skip 3 dc, (3 dc, ch 2, 3 dc) around corner ch loop, skip 3 dc, 3 dc in next space, skip 3 dc, 4 dc in next space, now work 13 sl sts along the diagonal of the square and work 1 sl st into 3rd ch at beginning of row. Cut yarn and draw end through last st.

SHOULDERS

With MC. With RS facing, insert hook around corner ch at neck and bring yarn through. Ch 1, 1 hdc around corner loop, (1 hdc between next dc) 6 times, 1 sl st in next space; turn. Skip 1 sl st, 1 sl st in each of the hdc around both loops; turn. Work 1 hdc around each space across. Cut yarn and draw end through last st.

You have now completed the right front shoulder. Work the same way to complete back left shoulder. For the left front shoulder and back right shoulder, begin on WS and complete as for other shoulders.

FINISHING

Place pieces, patted out to finished measurements, between damp towels and leave until completely dry. Seam shoulders.

Edging: With MC, beginning at lower back, insert hook around 1 st at corner of a square and bring yarn through.

Rnd 1 (RS): Ch 1, 1 hdc in each space (10 hdc for each square), 4 hdc around ch in each corner, 1 hdc in each sl st around both stitch loops along diagonals, end with 1 sl st into ch loop.

Rnd 2 (RS): Ch 1, 1 hdc in each space, increase 1 hdc in corner by working 2 hdc in center space, increase 1 hdc at lower part of the half square at neck and 1 decrease at top part of the half square. End with 1 sl st around ch.

Rnd 3 (RS): Work around in crab stitch (= single crochet worked from left to right). Hold the hook as for regular sc but insert the hook to the right of the stitch on the hook. Skip the first st and then work 1 crab st through both loops of each hdc. Cut yarn and draw end through last st. Weave in all ends neatly on WS.

ARMHOLE EDGINGS

Begin at the shoulder and work as for the vest edging. On the 2nd rnd, decrease 1 st at each underarm corner. Cut yarn and draw end through last st. Weave in all ends neatly on WS.

TIE FOR WAIST

Ch until cord is desired length. Turn and work 1 sl st in each ch. Cut yarn and draw end through last st. Thread cord through squares at waist (see photo page 87). Tie in a bow.

Hairband

Here's an easy to way dress up a hairband or decorate a crown. It's guaranteed to attract attention and add flair.

Yarn: CYCA #1 (sock/fingering/baby) Mandarin Petit (100% cotton, 195 yd/178 m / 50 g; *see page 142*)
Yarn Amounts: Leftover yarns in desired colors
Crochet Hook: U.S. size D-3 / 3 mm
Notions: simple, single-color hairband

The pattern depends on the size and width of the band. Ch 4 and join into a ring with 1 sl st into 1st ch. End all rnds with 1 sl st into 1st ch to complete rnd.
Rnd 1: Ch 1, work 6 sc around ring.
Rnd 2: Ch 1, (1 sc in next st, 2 sc in next st) around = 9 sts.
Rnd 3: Ch 1, 1 sc in each st around = 9 sts.
Repeat Rnd 3 until the band cover is long enough, insert band and then work the last two rounds:
Second-to-last Rnd: Ch 1, [1 sc, 2sctog (= insert hook into next st, yarn around hook and through st, hook through next st, yarn around hook and through st = 3 loops on hook; yarn around hook and through all 3 loops at once)] around = 6 sts rem.
Last Rnd: Ch 1, (2sctog) around = 3 sts rem.
Cut yarn and draw end through last st. Seam opening as necessary.
The band shown here is decorated with a "Flower in several layers with a solid center" (*see page 20*). The center of the flower has a crocheted bead (*see page 77*) sewn on.

For this accessory, I bought some hair clips and decorated them with various flowers and shapes. You can find similar solid color little clips in craft shops or other stores that sell accessories.

Choose something that suits you from the chapter "A Little Extra for Decoration," and embellish your hair clip with it. For these examples, I used:

Green clip: "Simple flowers 1 and 2" (*see page 22*).

Pink clip: "Butterfly" (*see page 26*).

Orange clip: "Simple flower 2" (*see page 22*), with a wooden bead at the center.

Cerise clip: "Butterfly" (*see page 26*).

Large bag

Crocheted bags are the perfect colorful accessory for summer. Crochet a solid color bag and dress it up with multi-colored flowers or crochet a striped bag that will make you happy every time you see it. Crocheting a bag isn't hard or tricky—just go for it and you'll have summer's most personal bag.

Yarn: CYCA #1 (sock/fingering/baby) Mandarin Petit (100% cotton, 195 yd/178 m / 50 g; *see page 142*)

Yarn Amounts: For white bag, approx. 400 g White 1001 and leftover yarns, or 50 g each for stripes. For striped bag, 150 g Turquoise 6705, 150 g Light Turquoise 6803, 100 g Pink 4505, and approx. 100 g White 1001 for stripes

Crochet Hook: U.S. size E-4 / 3.5 mm for a tighter fabric

Notions: Braided cord for the handles; matching sewing thread

NOTE: Hold yarn double throughout.

BASE

With two strands of yarn held together, ch 5 and join into a ring with 1 sl st in 1st ch. End every sc rnd with 1 sl st into 1st ch or end every dc rnd with 1 sl st into top of ch 3 to complete the rnd.

Rnd 1: Ch 1, 8 sc around ring = 8 sts.

Rnd 2: Ch 1, 2 sc in each st around = 16 sts.

Rnd 3: Ch 1, (1 sc in next st, 2 sc in next st) around = 24 sts.

Rnd 4: Ch 1, (1 sc in each of next 2 sts, 2 sc in next st) around = 32 sts.

Rnd 5: Ch 1, (1 sc in each of next 3 sts, 2 sc in next st) around = 40 sts.

Rnd 6: Ch 1, (1 sc in each of next 4 sts, 2 sc in next st) around = 48 sts.

Rnd 7: Ch 1, (1 sc in each of next 5 sts, 2 sc in next st) around = 56 sts.

Rnd 8: Ch 1, (1 sc in each of next 6 sts, 2 sc in next st) around = 64 sts.

Rnd 9: Ch 1, (1 sc in each of next 7 sts, 2 sc in next st) around = 72 sts.

Rnd 10: Ch 1, (1 sc in each of next 8 sts, 2 sc in next st) around = 80 sts.

Rnd 11: Ch 1, (1 sc in each of next 9 sts, 2 sc in next st) around = 88 sts.

Rnd 12: Ch 1, (1 sc in each of next 10 sts, 2 sc in next st) around = 96 sts.

Rnd 13: Ch 1, (1 sc in each of next 11 sts, 2 sc in next st) around = 104 sts.

Rnd 14: Ch 1, (1 sc in each of next 12 sts, 2 sc in next st) around = 112 sts.

Rnd 15: Ch 1, (1 sc in each of next 13 sts, 2 sc in next st) around = 120 sts.

Rnd 16: Ch 1, (1 sc in each of next 14 sts, 2 sc in next st) around = 128 sts.

Rnd 17: Ch 1, (1 sc in each of next 15 sts, 2 sc in next st) around = 136 sts.

The base is now complete; continue directly to the body of the bag.

BODY OF BAG

Rnd 1: Ch 1, (1 sc in each of next 16 sts, 2 sc in next st) around = 144 sts.

Rnds 2–4: Ch 1, 1 sc in each st around = 144 sts.

Rnd 5: Ch 1, (1 sc in each of next 17 sts, 2 sc in next st) around = 152 sts.

Rnd 6 (change to dc): Ch 3 = 1st dc, 1 dc in each st around = 152 sts.

Rnd 7 (return to single crochet): Ch 1, 1 sc in each st around = 152 sts.

Rnd 8: Ch 1, (1 sc in each of next 18 sts, 2 sc in next st) around = 160 sts.

Rnds 9–11: Ch 1, 1 sc in each st around = 160 sts.

Rnd 12: Ch 1, (1 sc in each of next 19 sts, 2 sc in next st) around = 168 sts.

Rnd 13 (change to dc): Ch 3 = 1st dc, 1 dc in each st around = 168 sts.

Rnd 14 (return to single crochet): Ch 1, 1 sc in each st around = 168 sts.

Rnd 15: Ch 1, (1 sc in each of next 20 sts, 2 sc in next st) around = 176 sts.

Rnds 16-19: Ch 1, 1 sc in each st around = 176 sts.

Rnd 20 (change to dc): Ch 3 = 1st dc, 1 dc in each st around = 176 sts.

Rnds 21-26 (return to single crochet): Ch 1, 1 sc in each st around = 176 sts.

Rnd 27 (change to dc): Ch 3 = 1st dc, 1 dc in each st around = 176 sts.

Rnds 28-33 (return to single crochet): Ch 1, 1 sc in each st around = 176 sts.

Rnd 34 (change to dc): Ch 3 = 1st dc, 1 dc in each st around = 176 sts).

Rnds 35-40 (return to single crochet): Ch 1, 1 sc in each st around = 176 sts.

Rnd 41 (change to dc): Ch 3 = 1st dc, 1 dc in each st around = 176 sts.

Rnds 42-47 (return to single crochet): Ch 1, 1 sc in each st around = 176 sts.

Rnd 48 (change to dc): Ch 3 = 1st dc, 1 dc in each st around = 176 sts.

Rnds 49-54 (return to single crochet): Ch 1, 1 sc in each st around = 176 sts.

Rnd 55 (change to dc): Ch 3 = 1st dc, 1 dc in each st around = 176 sts.

Rnds 56-61 (return to single crochet): Ch 1, 1 sc in each st around = 176 sts.

Rnd 62 (change to dc): Ch 3 = 1st dc, 1 dc in each st around = 176 sts.

Rnds 63-70 (return to single crochet): Ch 1, 1 sc in each st around = 176 sts.

Cut yarn and draw end through last st. Weave in all ends on WS.

Fold the edge down along the last dc round and sew down to WS with sewing thread.

For the white bag shown here, I changed colors on every round with dc in the instructions. On the turquoise and pink bag, I alternated between the two shades of turquoise and Pink on the single crochet rounds. Every round in dc was worked in White.

For my bags, I made the handles with braided cords. Yarn and hobby stores have ready-made handles that you can buy if you'd rather. You can even use simple crochet handles by chaining the desired number of sts and working sc back and forth until the width is the size you want. Securely sew the handles to the bag.

Yarn: CYCA #1 (sock/fingering/baby) Mandarin Petit (100% cotton, 195 yd/178 m / 50 g; *see page 142*)
Yarn Amounts: Approx. 150 g
Crochet Hook: U.S. size E-4 / 3.5 mm
Notions: Braided cord for the handles; matching sewing thread; wooden beads
NOTE: Hold yarn double throughout.

With two strands of yarn held together, ch 5 and join into a ring with 1 sl st in 1st ch. End every rnd with 1 sl st into 1st ch to complete the rnd.
Rnd 1: Ch 1, 8 sc around ring = 8 sts.
Rnd 2: Ch 1, 2 sc in each st around = 16 sts.
Rnd 3: Ch 1, (1 sc in next st, 2 sc in next st) around = 24 sts.
Rnd 4: Ch 1, (1 sc in each of next 2 sts, 2 sc in next st) around = 32 sts.

Rnd 5: Ch 1, (1 sc in each of next 3 sts, 2 sc in next st) around = 40 sts.
Rnd 6: Ch 1, (1 sc in each of next 4 sts, 2 sc in next st) around = 48 sts.
Rnd 7: Ch 1, (1 sc in each of next 5 sts, 2 sc in next st) around = 56 sts.
Rnd 8: Ch 1, (1 sc in each of next 6 sts, 2 sc in next st) around = 64 sts.
Rnd 9: Ch 1, 1 sc in each st around = 64 sts.
Rnd 10: Ch 1, (1 sc in each of next 7 sts, 2 sc in next st) around = 72 sts.
Rnd 11: Ch 1, 1 sc in each st around = 72 sts.
Rnd 12: Ch 1, (1 sc in each of next 8 sts, 2 sc in next st) around = 80 sts.
Rnds 13–43: Ch 1, 1 sc in each st around = 80 sts.
Rnd 44: Ch 1, work around the edge in crab stitch (single crochet worked from left to right). Cut yarn and draw end through last st. Weave in ends on WS.
For my bag, I made the handles with braided cords. Yarn and hobby stores have ready-made handles that you can buy if you'd rather. You can even make simple crocheted handles by chaining the desired number of sts and working sc back and forth until the width is the size you want. Securely sew the handles to the bag.
The bag shown here has a little decoration with 2 rounds of slip stitch on the RS, each in a different color. These two rounds substitute for Rnds 42 and 43 of the pattern. Some wooden beads were strung on a cord and tied around one of the handles.

Autumn Lovely and Winter Warm

AUTUMN IS THE PERFECT SEASON for curling up on the sofa and learning how to crochet. This chapter has both very easy projects and some more advanced ones to set your teeth into. The yarn for the projects is a cotton/merino wool blend that doesn't itch.

Adult size hat

This simple beret-style hat with a large flower on the side is easy to make.

Yarn: CYCA #3 (DK/light worsted) Sandnes Duo (55% Merino wool, 45% cotton, 136 yd/124 m / 50 g; *see page 142*)
Yarn Amount: Approx. 150 g
Crochet Hook: U.S. sizes H-8 / 5 mm for the hat and G-6 / 4 mm for the edging
NOTE: Hold yarn double throughout.

With two strands of yarn held together and larger size hook, ch 4 and join into a ring with 1 sl st into 1st ch. End every round with 1 sl st into 1st st to complete the round.
Rnd 1: Ch 1, 6 sc around ring = 6 sts.
Rnd 2: Ch 1, 2 sc in each st around = 12 sts.
Rnd 3: Ch 1, (1 sc in next st, 2 sc in next st) around = 18 sts.
Rnd 4: Ch 1, (1 sc in each of next 2 sts, 2 sc in next st) around = 24 sts.

Rnd 5: Ch 1, (1 sc in each of next 3 sts, 2 sc in next st) around = 30 sts.
Rnd 6: Ch 1, (1 sc in each of next 4 sts, 2 sc in next st) around = 36 sts.
Rnd 7: Ch 1, (1 sc in each of next 5 sts, 2 sc in next st) around = 42 sts.
Rnd 8: Ch 1, (1 sc in each of next 6 sts, 2 sc in next st) around = 48 sts.
Rnd 9: Ch 1, (1 sc in each of next 7 sts, 2 sc in next st) around = 54 sts.
Rnd 10: Ch 1, (1 sc in each of next 8 sts, 2 sc in next st) around = 60 sts.
Rnd 11: Ch 1, (1 sc in each of next 9 sts, 2 sc in next st) around = 66 sts.
Rnd 12: Ch 3 (= 1st dc), 2 dc in same st, (skip 2 sts, 3 dc in same st) around, end with 1 sl st into top of ch 3 at beginning of rnd.
Rnd 13: Ch 3, 2 dc in same space between dc groups, (3 dc in next space between dc groups) around. Repeat Rnd 13 for another 10 rounds (if you want a baggier hat, add more rounds here).
Now work the brim.

BRIM

Change to smaller size hook. Work 11 rnds (or to desired length): Ch 1, work 1 sc in each st around.

For the hat shown here, I worked 2 rnds of sl st in different colors as decoration. The hat was embellished with a "Flower in several layers" (*see page 18*).

Brimmed child's hat

The same model as the adult's hat but this version features a little peak in front (*see page 144*).

Yarn: CYCA #3 (DK/light worsted) Sandnes Duo (55% Merino wool, 45% cotton, 136 yd/124 m / 50 g; *see page 142*)

Yarn Amount: Approx. 150 g

Crochet Hook: U.S. size H-8 / 5 mm for the hat, U.S. size G-6 / 4 mm for the brim, and U.S. size E-4 / 3.5 mm for the peak

NOTE: Hold yarn double throughout.

With two strands of yarn held together and largest size hook, ch 4 and join into a ring with 1 sl st into 1st ch. End every round with 1 sl st into 1st st to complete the round.

Rnd 1: Ch 1, 6 sc around ring = 6 sts.

Rnd 2: Ch 1, 2 sc in each st around = 12 sts.

Rnd 3: Ch 1, (1 sc in next st, 2 sc in next st) around = 18 sts.

Rnd 4: Ch 1, (1 sc in each of next 2 sts, 2 sc in next st) around = 24 sts.

Rnd 5: Ch 1, (1 sc in each of next 3 sts, 2 sc in next st) around = 30 sts.

Rnd 6: Ch 1, (1 sc in each of next 4 sts, 2 sc in next st) around = 36 sts.

Rnd 7: Ch 1, (1 sc in each of next 5 sts, 2 sc in next st) around = 42 sts.

Rnd 8: Ch 1, (1 sc in each of next 6 sts, 2 sc in next st) around = 48 sts.

Rnd 9: Ch 1, (1 sc in each of next 7 sts, 2 sc in next st) around = 54 sts. Stop here if the hat is for a small child. If you want a larger size, increase as set for 1 or 2 more rounds.

Rnd 10: Change colors. Ch 3 (= 1st dc), 2 dc in same st, (skip 2 sts, 3 dc in same st) around; end with 1 sl st into top of ch 3 at beginning of rnd.

Rnd 11: Ch 3, 2 dc in same space between dc groups, (3 dc in next space between dc groups) around. Repeat Rnd 11 for another 9 rounds (if you want a baggier hat, add more rounds here).

Now work the brim.

BRIM

Change to medium size hook. Work approx. 8 rnds: Ch 1, 1 sc in each st around.

PEAK

Change to smallest size hook.

Row 1: Ch 1, work 26 sc along edge of hat; turn (26 sts).

Row 2: Ch 1, 26 sc; turn (26 sts).

Row 3: Ch 1, sc2tog (insert hook into next st, yarn around hook and through st, hook through next st, yarn around hook and through st = 3 loops on hook; yarn around hook and through all 3 loops at once)], 22 sc, sc2tog; turn = 24 sts.

Row 4: Ch 1, sc2tog, 1 sc in each of next 2 sts, 2 sc in next st, 14 sc, 2 sc in next st, 2 sc, sc2tog; turn = 24 sts.

Row 5: Ch 1, sc2tog, 1 sc, 2 sc in next st, 16 sc, 2 sc in next st, 1 sc, sc2tog; turn = 24sts.

Row 6: Ch 1, sc2tog, 1 sc, 2 sc in next st, 16 sc, 2 sc in next st, 1 sc, sc2tog = 24 sts.

Work in sc all round the edge of the peak and around rest of hat. I used another color here.

If you like, decorate the hat with a "Flower in several layers" (*see page 18*).

Beret

Here's a variation on the basic beret, worked in single crochet. It's shaped by working through the back loops only, instead of both loops, on some rows. The same basic hat is decorated totally differently. How will you embellish your hat?

Yarn: CYCA #3 (DK/light worsted) Sandnes Duo (55% Merino wool, 45% cotton, 136 yd/124 m / 50 g; *see page 142*)

Yarn Amount: Approx. 150 g

Crochet Hook: U.S. size J-10 / 6 mm for both sizes + H-8 / 5 mm for adult size and U.S. size G-6 / 4 mm for child's size

NOTE: Hold yarn double throughout.

With two strands of yarn held together and J-10 / 6 mm hook, ch 4 and join into a ring with 1 sl st into 1st ch. End every round with 1 sl st into 1st st to complete the round.

Rnd 1: Ch 1, 6 sc around ring = 6 sts.

Rnd 2: Ch 1, 2 sc in each st around = 12 sts.

Rnd 3: Ch 1, (1 sc in next st, 2 sc in next st) around = 18 sts.

Rnd 4: Ch 1, (1 sc in each of next 2 sts, 2 sc in next st) around = 24 sts.

Rnd 5 (sc in back loops only): Ch 1, (1 sc in each of next 3 sts, 2 sc in next st) around = 30 sts.

Rnd 6: Ch 1, (1 sc in each of next 4 sts, 2 sc in next st) around = 36 sts.

Rnd 7 (sc in back loops only): Ch 1, (1 sc in each of next 5 sts, 2 sc in next st) around = 42 sts.

Rnd 8: Ch 1, (1 sc in each of next 6 sts, 2 sc in next st) around = 48 sts.

Rnd 9 (sc in back loops only): Ch 1, (1 sc in each of next 7 sts, 2 sc in next st) around = 54 sts.

Rnd 10: Ch 1, (1 sc in each of next 8 sts, 2 sc in next st) around = 60 sts.

Rnd 11 (sc in back loops only): Ch 1, (1 sc in each of next 9 sts, 2 sc in next st) around = 66 sts.

Rnd 12: Ch 1, (1 sc in each of next 10 sts, 2 sc in next st) around = 72 sts.

Rnd 13 (sc in back loops only): Ch 1, (1 sc in each of next 11 sts, 2 sc in next st) around = 78 sts.

Rnd 14: Ch 1, (1 sc in each of next 12 sts, 2 sc in next st) around = 84 sts.

Rnd 15 (sc in back loops only): Ch 1, (1 sc in each of next 13 sts, 2 sc in next st) around = 90 sts.

Rnd 16: Ch 1, (1 sc in each of next 14 sts, 2 sc in next st) around = 96 sts.

Rnd 17 (sc in back loops only): Ch 1, (1 sc in each of next 15 sts, 2 sc in next st) around = 102 sts.

Rnds 18-22 (working odd-number rnds in back loops only): Ch 1, 1 sc in each st around = 102 sts.

Rnd 23 (sc in back loops only): Ch 1, [15 sc, sc2tog in next st (insert hook into next st, yarn around hook and through st, hook through next st, yarn around hook and through st = 3 loops on hook; yarn around hook and through all 3 loops at once)] around = 96 sts rem.

Rnd 24: Ch 1, (14 sc, sc2tog in next st) around = 90 sts rem.

Rnd 25 (sc in back loops only): Ch 1, [13 sc, sc2tog in next st) around = 84 sts rem.

Rnd 26: Ch 1, (12 sc, sc2tog in next st) around = 78 sts rem.

Rnd 27 (sc in back loops only): Ch 1, [11 sc, sc2tog in next st) around = 72 sts rem.

Rnd 28: Ch 1, (10 sc, sc2tog in next st) around = 66 sts rem.

Change to smaller size hook depending on how tight you want the hat. For a smaller child (3-4 years), use hook U.S. G-6 / 4 mm. If you want a larger size that could even fit an adult (depending on how big the head is), use U.S. H-8 / 5 mm.

Rnds 29-36: Ch 1, 1 sc in each st around (66 sts). Cut yarn and draw end through last st.

If you like, decorate the hat with 1 rnd sl st on the RS between the 6th and 7th rnds above the last round.

The two examples shown here were also embellished as follows:

One of the hats has a large "Flower in several layers with a 'wheel' at the center" (*see instructions on page 18*).

The other hat has lots of little flowers decorating it (see instructions below).

LITTLE FLOWER

Ch 4 and join into a ring with 1 sl st into 1st ch.

Rnd 1: Ch 1, work 10 sc around ring; end with 1 sl st into 1st ch.

Rnd 2: Ch 1, (1 sl st, 3 dc in next st) around and end with 1 sl st into 1st ch. Cut yarn, leaving tail long enough to sew flower on.

Lamb's ear hat with bobbles

"What on earth is a bobble?" you might wonder. Crocheted bobbles are fun and provide some structure. They are groups of stitches gathered together into little bumps that stick up from the crochet surface. This is a wonderfully sweet little hat for the littlest ones. It fits down over small ears and can be tied under the chin.

Size: 1-3 years
Yarn: CYCA #3 (DK/light worsted) Sandnes Duo (55% Merino wool, 45% cotton, 136 yd/124 m / 50 g; *see page 142*)
Yarn Amounts: Approx. 150 g for the hat and leftover yarns or a skein of each color for the inner ears and flower
Crochet Hook: U.S. sizes G-6 and H-8 / 4 and 5 mm
NOTE: Hold yarn double throughout.

The hat is worked in one piece and crocheted together when finished to shape it correctly. It begins with ribbing for the front edge.

With smaller size hook and two strands of yarn held together, ch 5.
Row 1: Beginning in 2nd ch from hook, work 1 sc in each ch across, end with ch 1; turn.
Rows 2-58: Work 1 sc in back loop only of each st and end row with ch 1; turn.
The ribbing is now complete and should be turned lengthwise. Continue as follows:

Row 1: Change to larger size hook and work dc evenly spaced across with 1 dc in each row down one long edge of ribbed band: begin with ch 2 and work dc across = 58 dc. Ch 2; turn.
Row 2: Work 1 dc in each st across and end with ch 2; turn.
Row 3 with bobbles: Work 5 dc and then make a bobble as follows:
A bobble consists of 5 dc worked into the same st, but each dc is worked as: *yarn around hook, insert hook into st, yarn around hook and through st, yarn around hook

and through 2 loops on the hook. Repeat from * 3 more times and then yarn around hook, insert hook and bring yarn through without going through 2 loops on the hook. There should now be 7 loops on the hook. Yarn around hook and through all 7 loops at the same time. You have now made 5 dc into 1 st. Repeat (1 dc in each of next 5 sts, 1 bobble) across, ending with 4 dc, ch 2.

Row 4: Work across in dc and end with ch 2; turn.

Row 5 with bobbles: Work 2 dc, 1 bobble, 1 dc in each of next 5 sts, 1 bobble) across, ending with 1 dc and ch 2; turn. Staggering the bobbles makes an attractive pattern.

Repeat Rows 2-5 for a total of 10 rows.

On the last two rows, Rows 11 and 12, increase 2 sts at the center of the hat before it will be joined. This is the tip of the hat.

Row 11: Work as for Row 5 with bobbles and, after 29 sts (including the bobbles), work 3 dc in the next st. Continue across in pattern, making sure that the bobbles align in the staggered pattern (count the 3 dc at center as 1 st when calculating the stitch pattern). End with ch 2; turn.

Row 12: Work 30 dc and then 3 dc into same st. Continue with 30 dc; do not turn.

CROCHETING HAT TOGETHER

Turn the hat so WS is facing out and the bobbles face in. Work sc through the stitch loops of both sides down center back. Cut yarn and draw end through last st. Now extend the ribbing, beginning at each short end to make long ties:

Work 27 rows: Sc through back loops of 4 sts across, ch 1; turn. On the last row, sc2tog twice. Cut yarn and draw end through last st.

For the hat shown in the photo on page 102, I worked across the space between the ribbing and 1st row of hat in slip stitch for a decorative effect. The hat was also embellished with a "Flower in several layers with a 'wheel' at the center" (*see instructions on page 18*).

EARS

Make two ears alike. Each ear has two parts, each in a different color, that are sewn together and then sewn onto the hat below its tip.

INNER EAR (PINK)

With U.S. size G-6 / 4 mm hook and two strands of pink yarn held together, ch 4 and join into a ring with 1 sl st into 1st ch.

Row 1: Ch 1, 7 sc around ring; end with 1 sl st into 1st ch; turn = 7 sts.

Row 2: Work 1 sc into each of next 3 sts, 3 sc into next st, 1 sc into each of next 3 sts and end with ch 1 and turn = 9 sts.

Row 3: Work 1 sc into each of next 4 sts, 3 sc into next st, 1 sc in each of next 4 sts; end with ch 1 and turn = 11 sts.

Row 4: Work (1 sc, 2 sc in next sc, 1 sc in each of next 2 sts, 2 sc in next sc) twice; 1 sc; end with ch 1 and turn = 15 sts.

Row 5: Work 1 sc into each of next 6 sts, 2 sc in next st, 1 sc, 2 sc in next st, 1 sc in each of next 6 sts; end with ch 1 and turn = 17 sts.

Continued on page 144

Scarves

Scarves are rewarding to crochet. There is no shaping or measuring; just crochet until the scarf is as large as you want.

Here are three variations of scarves in different techniques. Which is your favorite?

CIRCULAR SCARF

This scarf is worked in one piece, around and around until it is the desired width. You can wrap it in one or two figure eights around your neck. It's so fine and simple.

Yarn: CYCA #3 (DK/light worsted) Sandnes Duo (55% Merino wool, 45% cotton, 136 yd/124 m / 50 g; *see page 142*)
Yarn Amount: Approx. 250 g
Crochet Hook: U.S. size J-10 / 6 mm
NOTE: Hold yarn double throughout.

With two strands of yarn held together, ch 250 and join into a ring with 1 sl st into 1st ch. Make sure that the foundation chain is not twisted when you join.
Rnd 1: Ch 1, 1 sc, (ch 1, skip 1 st, 1 sc) around and end with 1 sl st into 1st ch.
Rnd 2: Ch 1, (1 sc in ch loop of previous rnd, ch 1, skip 1 st) around and end with 1 sl st into 1st ch.
Rnds 3–20: Ch 1, (1 sc in ch loop of previous rnd, ch 1) around and end with 1 sl st into 1st ch. After completing Rnd 20, cut yarn and draw end through last st. Weave in ends on WS.

This scarf can be decorated with a "Loopy flower" (*see page 21*).

FLOWERY SCARF

This scarf is composed of many flowers crocheted together at the flower petal tips on the last round. Use several colors and repeat the pattern four times.

Yarn: CYCA #3 (DK/light worsted) Sandnes Duo (55% Merino wool, 45% cotton, 136 yd/124 m / 50 g; *see page 142*)
Yarn Amount: Depends on how many colors you use and how large you make the scarf. The example shown here used 100 g each of four different colors.
Crochet Hook: U.S. size G-6 / 4 mm

FLOWER

Ch 5 and join into a ring with 1 sl st into 1st ch.
Rnd 1: Ch 2 (= 1st dc), 17 dc around ring; end with 1 sl st into top of ch 2 at beginning of rnd.
Rnd 2: (Ch 5, skip 2 sts and work 1 sc in the 3rd st) 5 times and end with ch 5, 1 sl st into 1st ch at beginning of rnd.
Rnd 3, Flower Petals: (1 sc, 1 hdc, 2 dc, 1 tr, 2 dc, 1 hdc, 1 sc around ch loop) 6 times; end with 1 sl st into 1st sc. Cut yarn and draw end through last st.
The flowers are joined at the tip of each petal in the treble st. Join the flowers with 1 sc and finish petal as set. Finish by weaving in all ends on WS.

GRANNY SQUARE SCARF

This scarf consists of many squares crocheted together—a fun variation of the granny square with a "wheel" at the center. Choose your favorite colors and make fall's coziest scarf.

Yarn: CYCA #3 (DK/light worsted) Sandnes Duo (55% Merino wool, 45% cotton, 136 yd/124 m / 50 g; *see page 142*)

Crochet Hook: U.S. size H-8 / 5 mm

NOTE: Hold yarn double throughout.

SQUARE

With two strands of yarn held together, ch 4 and join into a ring with 1 sl st into 1st ch. End all rnds with 1 sl st into top of ch 2 at beginning of rnd.

Rnd 1: Ch 2 (= 1st dc), 11 dc around ring = 12 sts.

Rnd 2: Ch 2, 1 dc in same space, 2 dc in each space between dc of previous rnd = 24 sts.

Rnd 3: Ch 2, 2 dc in same space, 3 dc in each space between dc of previous rnd, but, on every 3rd space, form a corner: (3 dc, ch 1, 3 dc) into space.

When you are on the last rnd of the next square, join it along one side to the first square (*see instructions on page 14*).

You can make the scarf as long as you like. The example shown here has 16 squares and the last square is joined only at the corners to make a slot to slip the scarf end through.

When all of the squares have been crocheted and joined, work an edging of sc around the scarf. At each corner, work 3 sc into corner st. Work the first rnd of sc edging with gray yarn and the second round with red. Cut yarn and weave in all ends on WS.

Spray the scarf with water and lightly steam press so the scarf lies flat.

Adult size slippers

Yarn: CYCA #3 (DK/light worsted) Sandnes Duo (55% Merino wool, 45% cotton, 136 yd/124 m / 50 g; *see page 142*)

Yarn Amounts: 50 g for the sole, 100 g for the top

Crochet Hook: U.S. size G-6 / 4 mm

Notions: 2 buttons; matching sewing thread

SOLE

Ch 28 (29, 30, 31, 32). All rnds end with 1 sl st into 1st ch at beginning of rnd.

Rnd 1: Beginning in 2nd from hook, work 26 (27, 28, 29, 30) sc and, in last st, work 3 sc; turn and work 25 (26, 27, 28, 29) sc along opposite side of foundation chain, and, in the last st which already has 1 sc, work 2 more sc.

Rnd 2: Ch 1, work 2 sc in 1st st, 25 (26, 27, 28, 29) sc, (2 sc in next st) 3 times, 25 (26, 27, 28, 29) sc, 2 sc in next st, 1 sc.

Rnd 3: Ch 1, 1 sc, 2 sc in next st, 25 (26, 27, 28, 29) sc, 2 sc in next st, 1 sc, 2 sc in next st, 1 sc, 2 sc in next st, 26 (27, 28, 29, 30) sc, 2 sc in next st, 2 sc.

Rnd 4: Ch 1, 2 sc, 2 sc in next st, 26 (27, 28, 29, 30) sc, 2 sc in next st, 2 sc, 2 sc in next st st, 2 sc, 2 sc in next st, 26 (27, 28, 29, 30) sc, 2 sc in next st, 3 sc.

Rnd 5: Ch 1, 3 sc, 2 sc in next st, 27 (28, 29, 30, 31) sc, 2 sc in next st, 3 sc, 2 sc in next st, 3 sc, 2 sc in next st, 26 (27, 28, 29, 30) sc, 2 sc in next st, 4 sc.

Rnd 6: Ch 1, 4 sc, 2 sc in next st, 11 (12, 13, 14, 15) sc, 3 hdc, 12 dc, 2 dc in next st, 1 dc, 2 dc in next st, 2 dc, 2 dc in next st, 1 dc, 2 dc in next st, 1 dc, 2 dc in next st, 2 dc, 2 dc in next st, 12 dc, 3 hdc, 11 (12, 13, 14, 15) sc, 2 sc in next sc,

5 sc. Cut yarn and draw end through last st.

TOP

End all rnds with 1 sl st into 1st ch or top of ch 2.

Rnd 7: Change colors and begin at the center back of the sole. With WS facing up, work 1 rnd of sl st around last rnd of sole.

Rnd 8: Ch 2 (= 1st hdc), work 1 hdc in each sl st around. Mark the center 28 sts at the toe). End with 1 sl st into top of ch 2 at beginning of rnd.

Rnd 9: Ch 1, 1 sc in each st around except the marked 28 sts at center—over these sts, work dc2tog 14 times (dc2tog = *yarn around hook, hook through next st, yarn around hook and through st, yarn around hook and through 2 loops on hook*; repeat from * to * and then yarn around hook and through rem 3 loops).

Rnd 10: Ch 1, 1 sc in each st around.

Rnd 11: Ch 1, 1 sc in each st around; mark 12 sts at center.

Rnd 12: Ch 1, 1 sc in each st around except for the 12 center sts—dc3tog 4 times and then mark 8 sts at center.

Rnd 13: Ch 1, 1 sc in each st around except the marked center sts—dc2tog 4 times. Mark center 30 sts at heel.

Rnd 14: Ch 2, work 1 dc in each st to 1st marked st, ch 2, sl st in each st to next marker, ch 2, work 1 dc in each of rem sts to end of rnd. End with 1 sl st into top of ch 2 at beginning of rnd. Cut yarn and draw end through last st.

ANKLE STRAPS

Row 1: With RS facing, insert hook into 1st dc at heel

marker at side of the slipper (see Rnd 14) and work sc around dc from previous rnd.

Row 2: *For the right slipper*, make a strip: Ch 20, 1 sc in 2nd ch from hook and in next st, ch 2, skip 2 sts (for buttonhole), 1 sc in each st to end of strip, slip st in each sc directly over Row 1 back to the other side of the ankle. Cut yarn and draw end through last st.

For the left slipper, work Row 1 first and turn, sl st in each st directly over Row 1 back to the other side of the ankle, ch 20, sc in 2nd ch from hook and 1 sc in next st, ch 2, skip 2 sts (for buttonhole), 1 sc in each st to other side of strip, 1 sl st in each sc directly over Row 1 back to the other side of the ankle, cut yarn and draw end through last st. Sew on buttons.

The slippers shown here are decorated with 1 rnd sl st in a contrasting color around the top edge (see photo for stripe placement) + a "Flower in several layers with a solid center"—2 layers used (*see instructions on page 20*).

Child's slippers

Aren't these just so sweet? These slippers may be a little too slippery for small children; you can find skid-proof rubber latex soles in many craft and yarn shops.

Sizes: Approx. 1 (2) years
Yarn: CYCA #3 (DK/light worsted) Sandnes Duo (55% Merino wool, 45% cotton, 136 yd/124 m / 50 g; *see page 142*)
Yarn Amounts: 50 g for the sole (Color 1), approx. 50 g for the top (Color 2)
Crochet Hook: U.S. size G-6 / 4 mm
Notions: 2 buttons; matching sewing thread
NOTE: Hold yarn double throughout.

SOLE

With 2 strands of Color 1 held together, ch 15 (18).
Rnd 1: Work 2 sc in 2nd ch from hook, 8 (11) sc, 4 hdc, 4 hdc in last st. Turn and work into loops of opposite side of foundation chain: 4 hdc, 8 (11) sc, 2 sc in last st which already has 2 sc in it from beginning of rnd. End with 1 sl st into 1st sc = 32 (38) sts.
Rnd 2: Ch 1, 2 sc in each of next 2 sts, 7 (10), sc, 5 hdc, 2 hdc in each of next 4 sts, 5 hdc, 7 (10) sc, 2 sc in each of next 2 sts. End with 1 sl st into 1st ch = 40 (46) sts.
Rnd 3: Ch 2, 1 hdc, 2 hdc in next st, 14 (17) hdc, 2 hc in next st, 1 hdc, 2 sc in next st, 2 sc, 2 sc in next st, 1 hdc, 2 hdc in next st, 14 (17) hdc, 2 hdc in next st, 1 hdc. End with 1 sl st into top of ch 2 = 46 (52) sts.

Rnd 4: Work 1 sl st into each st around. Cut yarn and draw end through last st.

TOP

Rnd 5: Change to Color 2 (two strands held together) and attach at center back of sole. Ch 1 and then work 1 sc into each sl st around. Make sure you are only working through the slip sts of previous rnd. End with 1 sl st into 1st ch = 46 (52) sts.
Rnd 6: Ch 1, 15 (18) sc, (2 sc in next st, 2 sc) 5 times, 2 sc in next st, 15 (18) sc. End with 1 sl st into 1st ch = 52 (58) sts.
Rnd 7: Ch 1, 12 (15) sc, (1 sc in back loop, 2 sc) 9 times, 1 sc in back loop, 12 (15) sc; end with 1 sl st into 1st ch = 52 (58) sts.
Rnd 8: Ch 2, 1 hdc, hdc2tog (work as for regular hdc but draw yarn only through 2 loops of 1st hdc; begin 1 hdc in next st and bring yarn through all loops on hook), 2 (5) hdc, 7 sc, (1 sc in back loop, skip 1 st, 1 sc) 9 times, 1 sc in back loop, 7 sc, 2 (5) hdc, hdc2tog, 1 hdc. End with 1 sl st into top of ch 2 = 41 (47) sts.
Rnd 9: Ch 2, 1 hdc, hdc2tog, 1 hdc, 7 (10) sc, (1 sc in back loop, skip 1 st) 9 times, 1 sc in back loop, 7 (10) sc, 1 hdc, hdc2tog, 1 hdc. End with 1 sl st into top of ch 2 = 30 (36) sts.
Rnd 10: Ch 1, 1 sc in each st around; end with 1 sl st into 1st ch. Cut yarn and draw end through last st.
With a contrast color, work 1 rnd of sl st.
These slippers were decorated with "Simple flower 1" (*see page 22*).

FOOT STRAPS

Make 2 alike: With 2 strands of a contrast color, ch 10; work 1 sc in 4th ch from hook and then 6 sc across. Cut yarn and draw end through last st.

Securely sew one side of strap to each slipper, at slip st row. Securely sew on button at opposite side. Don't forget to sew the second strap on the other slipper to mirror-image the first one. Weave in all ends on WS. Attach skid-proof rubber latex soles if desired.

Children's crocheted boots

Sweet, warm, and pretty boots for little feet to wear in the winter. These boots may be a little too slippery for small children; you can find skid-proof rubber latex soles in many craft and yarn shops.

Sizes: Approx. 1 (2) years
Yarn: CYCA #3 (DK/light worsted) Sandnes Duo (55% Merino wool, 45% cotton, 136 yd/124 m / 50 g; *see page 142*)
Yarn Amounts: 50 g for the sole (Color 1), approx. 150 g for the top and leg (Color 2)
Crochet Hook: U.S. size G-6 / 4 mm
Notions: Imitation suede cord
NOTE: Hold yarn double throughout.

SOLE

With 2 strands of Color 1 held together, ch 15 (18).
Rnd 1: Work 2 sc in 2nd ch from hook, 8 (11) sc, 4 hdc, 4 hdc in last st. Turn and work into loops on opposite side of foundation chain: 4 hdc, 8 (11) sc, 2 sc in last st which already has 2 sc in it from beginning of rnd. End with 1 sl st into 1st sc = 32 (38) sts.
Rnd 2: Ch 1, 2 sc in each of next 2 sts, 7 (10) sc, 5 hdc, 2 hdc in each of next 4 sts, 5 hdc, 7 (10) sc, 2 sc in each of next 2 sts. End with 1 sl st into 1st ch = 40 (46) sts.
Rnd 3: Ch 2, 1 hdc, 2 hdc in next st, 14 (17) hdc, 2 hdc in next st, 1 hdc, 2 sc in next st, 2 sc, 2 sc in next st, 1 hdc, 2 hdc in next st, 14 (17) hdc, 2 hdc in next st, 1 hdc. End with 1 sl st into top of ch 2 = 46 (52) sts.
Rnd 4: Work 1 sl st into each st around. Cut yarn and draw end through last st.

TOP

Rnd 5: Change to Color 2 (two strands held together) and attach at center back of sole. Ch 1 and then work 1 sc into each sl st around. Make sure you are only working through the slip sts of previous rnd. End with 1 sl st into 1st ch = 46 (52) sts.
Rnds 6–8: Ch 1, work 1 sc in each st around. End with 1 sl st into 1st ch = 46 (52) sts.
Rnd 9: Ch 1, sc2tog in next st (insert hook into next st, yarn around hook and through st, hook through next st, yarn around hook and through st = 3 loops on hook; yarn around hook and through all 3 loops at once), 17 (20) sc, (sc2tog, 2 sc) 2 times, sc2tog, 17 (20) sc. End with 1 sl st into 1st ch = 42 (48) sts.
Rnd 10: Ch 1, 15 (18) sc, sc2tog, 1 sc, sc2tog, 2 sc, sc2tog, 1 sc, sc2tog, 15 (18) sc. End with 1 sl st into 1st ch = 38 (44) sts.
Rnd 11: Ch 1, 13 (16) sc, sc2tog, 1 sc, sc2tog, 2 sc, sc2tog, 1 sc, sc2tog, 13 (16) sc. End with 1 sl st into 1st ch = 34 (40) sts. Cut yarn and draw end through last st.
Rnd 12: Count out 11 (14) sts from center back of the boot. Attach yarn in the 12th (15th) st, inserting hook from

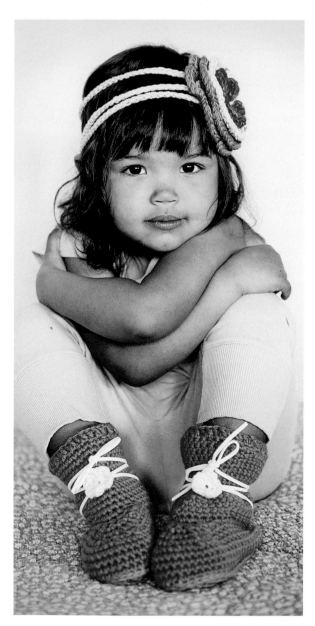

the inside, and work towards the toe. Ch 1, (sc2tog) 6 times; turn.

Rnd 13: Ch 1, 1 sc, skip 1 st, 2 sc, skip 1 st, 1 sc (now you are back where you started), ch 1, 26 (32) sc around. End with 1 sl st into 1st ch.

LEG

Rnds 14–24: Ch 1, work 1 sc in each st around. End with 1 sl st into 1st ch = 26 (32) sts.

Rnd 25: Ch 2, alternate (1 dc in front loop, 1 dc in back loop) around. End with 1 sl st into top of ch 2 at beginning of rnd. Cut yarn and draw end through last st. Weave in all ends on WS and thread imitation suede cord through at ankle (see photo). Attach skid-proof rubber latex soles if desired.

The boots were decorated with a "Simple flower 1" (*see instructions on page 22*). Sew a flower to the front of each boot.

You can make the flower hair band with a "Flower in several layers with a 'wheel' at the center" (*see page 18*) and some chain stitch cords. For both the flower and cords, use two strands of Sandnes Duo yarn held together and a hook that's U.S. size G-6 / 4 mm. Chain the number of stitches needed to fit comfortably about the head. Securely sew the band to the back of the flower.

Leg warmers

ADULT-SIZE LEG WARMERS

Yarn: CYCA #3 (DK/light worsted) Sandnes Duo (55% Merino wool, 45% cotton, 136 yd/124 m / 50 g; *see page 142*)

Yarn Amounts: 150 g

Crochet Hook: U.S. size H-8 / 5 mm

Ch 6.

Rows 1-43: Beginning in 2nd ch from hook, work 1 sc through back loops only in each ch across.

Fold the strip with RS facing RS and crochet the short ends together with sc through both layers. The ribbed cuff is now complete.

Attach yarn at edge and ch 2 (= 1st dc) then work 50 dc evenly spaced around; end with 1 sl st into top of ch 2 at beginning of rnd.

Change colors and alternate 1 round sc, 1 round dc. Begin sc rnds with ch 1 and dc rnds with ch 2. End each sc rnd with 1 sl st into 1st ch and each dc rnd with 1 sl st into top of ch 2. Work about 34 rnds the same way. On the last rnd, before the color change, work (1 sc in each of next 6 sts, sc2tog), end with 2 sc.

End with 3 rnds sc in the same color as for ribbing. Cut yarn and draw end through last st. Weave in all ends on WS.

The leg warmers shown in the photo to left on page 113 are decorated with a large flower constructed from 3 smaller flowers:

"Simple flower 1" (*see page 22*).

"Simple flower 2" (*see page 22*).

"Simple flower 3" (*see page 22*).

CHILD-SIZE LEG WARMERS

Yarn: CYCA #3 (DK/light worsted) Sandnes Duo (55% Merino wool, 45% cotton, 136 yd/124 m / 50 g; *see page 142*)

Yarn Amounts: 50 g of each color. I used 4 colors: Light Pink 4312, Pink 2 4616, Lilac 4823, and Dark Lilac 4762

Crochet Hook: U.S. size E-4 / 3.5 mm

Ch 61.

Row 1: Beginning in 2nd ch from hook, work 1 sc in each st across; turn.

Rows 2-37: Ch 1, 1 sc through back loop of each st across.

Color sequence: After every 2 rows, I changed color, working with 4 different colors.

Fold the piece with RS facing RS, aligning edges, and join with sc through both layers down leg. Cut yarn and draw end through last st. Weave in all ends on WS.

These legwarmers were decorated with "Simple flower 3" (see page 22).

Ribbed hat

These hats really are the easiest things one can crochet, the world's best beginner projects that still look professionally made. You don't need to worry about increasing or decreasing or any complicated calculations. You just crochet!

Sizing can easily be adjusted. Start with more chain stitches if you want a longer hat and work more rows if you want a wider one. The width also depends on how tight you want the hat.

RIBBED HAT WITH RABBIT POMPOM (Photo 1)

This loose-fitting hat is sized for adults.

Yarn: CYCA #3 (DK/light worsted) Sandnes Duo (55% Merino wool, 45% cotton, 136 yd/124 m / 50 g; *see page 142*)
Yarn Amounts: Approx. 100 g depending on size
Crochet Hook: U.S. size D-3 / 3 mm

Ch 61.
Row 1: Beginning in 2nd ch from hook, work 1 sc in each st across; turn.
Rows 2–99: Ch 1, 1 sc through back loop of each st across; turn.
After working 99 rows, fold the hat with RS facing RS, aligning edges, and join with sc through both layers. Cut yarn and draw end through last st.
Thread a length of yarn through the top of the hat, zigzagging across; pull tight and secure. Weave in all ends on WS.

I bought the rabbit pompom at a yarn store and attached it with the snap included with the pompom. I also embellished the hat with several colors of "Simple Flowers 1-3" (*see page 22*). Sew on flowers wherever you like on the hat.

RIBBED HAT WITH POMPOM (Photo 2)

This hat was crocheted in the same size for a two-year-old and a seven-year-old. It's loose and baggy.

Yarn: CYCA #3 (DK/light worsted) Sandnes Duo (55% Merino wool, 45% cotton, 136 yd/124 m / 50 g; *see page 142*)
Yarn Amounts: Approx. 100 g depending on size
Crochet Hook: U.S. size H-8 / 5 mm
NOTE: Hold yarn double throughout.

With two strands of yarn held together, ch 45.
Row 1: Beginning in 2nd ch from hook, work 1 sc in each st across; turn.
Rows 2–59: Ch 1, 1 sc through back loop of each st across; turn.
After working 59 rows, fold the hat with RS facing RS, aligning edges, and join with sc through both layers. Cut yarn and draw end through last st.
In the hat shown here, I worked a line of slip stitch in a contrast color down one side. Thread a length of yarn through the top of the hat, zigzagging across; pull tight

and secure. Weave in all ends on WS.

This hat is topped with a pompom. You can easily make a pompom with a pompom maker from the craft store or with 2 circles of stiff paper. Cut out a small circle at the center of each piece, like a doughnut hole. Hold the circles together and wrap the yarn around and around, through the holes—threading yarn onto a tapestry needle makes it easier—until the circles are completely filled. Cut yarn around outer edge and firmly tie a strong thread between the circles and around the ball to secure it. Remove the paper circles and trim ball evenly, but be careful not to trim too much! Steaming also fluffs up the pompom (be sure to protect your hands). Securely sew the pompom to the top of the hat. It's easy to vary the size of your pompoms by making larger or smaller circles.

RIBBED HAT WITH PINK BAND *(Photo 3)*

This rather tightly fitted hat is sized for a two-year-old.

Yarn: CYCA #3 (DK/light worsted) Sandnes Duo (55% Merino wool, 45% cotton, 136 yd/124 m / 50 g; *see page 142*)
Yarn Amounts: Approx. 100 g depending on size
Crochet Hook: U.S. size D-3 / 3 mm

Notions: Imitation suede cord

Ch 83.

Row 1: Beginning in 2nd ch from hook, work 1 sc in each st across; turn.

Rows 2–71: Ch 1, 1 sc through back loop of each st across; turn.

After working 71 rows, fold the hat with RS facing RS, aligning edges, and join with sc through both layers. Cut yarn and draw end through last st. Fold up the edge on one end and thread a cord through every other row on the other side and pull tight. In this case, the suede cord was threaded in 20 sts from the edge. The flower is composed of three crocheted circles that are stacked and sewn securely to the hat.

CIRCLE 1

Ch 4 and join into a ring with 1 sl st into 1st ch.

Rnd 1: Ch 2 (= 1st dc), work 11 dc around ring. End with 1 sl st into top of ch 2 at beginning of rnd.

CIRCLE 2

Ch 4 and join into a ring with 1 sl st into 1st ch.

Continued on page 144

Half gloves in ribbed crochet

Pretty little half gloves with an opening for the thumb. It might be a good just-big-enough project for someone who wants to learn how to crochet. It's easy to adjust sizing for half gloves. Add more stitches to the chain if you want a wider cuff and more rows if you want them longer.

These wrist warmers are sized for a seven-year-old, but it would be wise to measure before you start to make sure the sizing will be correct.

Yarn: CYCA #3 (DK/light worsted) Sandnes Duo (55% Merino wool, 45% cotton, 136 yd/124 m / 50 g; *see page 142*)

Yarn Amounts: Approx. 50 g depending on size; small amount of contrast color

Crochet Hook: U.S. size D-3 / 3 mm

Ch 41.

Row 1: Beginning in 2nd ch from hook, work 1 sc in each st across; turn.

Rows 2-35: Ch 1, 1 sc through back loop of each st across; turn.

Row 36: Change colors and work 1 sc through *both* loops around. Cut yarn and draw end through last st. Turn piece and, on opposite side, work 1 row of sc with the contrast color. This way, you will have an edging with the contrast color on both sides.

Fold the mitt with WS facing WS, aligning edges, and join with sc through both layers, leaving space for the

thumb. You will need to do a little measuring here: The mitts shown here are joined for 1¾ in / 4.5 cm below the thumb and 3½ in / 9 cm above it. The thumbhole is 1 in / 2.5 cm long.

I crocheted a round of slip st 11 rows from the top edge, in the same color as for the edgings. Instead of weaving in the ends, I left longer ends to tie into a bow.

It's easy to adjust the sizing on these wrist warmers. Add more stitches to the chain if you want a longer cuff and more rows if you want looser cuffs. These wrist warmers are sized for a two-year-old.

Yarn: CYCA #3 (DK/light worsted) Sandnes Duo (55% Merino wool, 45% cotton, 136 yd/124 m / 50 g; *see page 142*)
Yarn Amounts: Approx. 100 g depending on size
Crochet Hook: U.S. size D-3 / 3 mm
Notions: Imitation suede cord

Ch 36.
Row 1: Beginning in 2nd ch from hook, work 1 sc in each st across; turn.
Rows 2–29: Ch 1, 1 sc through back loop of each st across; turn.
After working 29 rows, fold the wrist warmer with RS facing RS, aligning edges, and join with sc through both layers. Cut yarn and draw end through last st.
Fold up the edge on one end. Thread the suede cord through every other row around the wrist and tie ends in a bow. These wrist warmers have the cord threaded 8 sts in from the edge.

WRIST WARMERS FOR AN ADULT

These wrist warmers are so easy to crochet and they look so fine. They are nice to have when it starts getting a little chilly outside but will even keep your hands

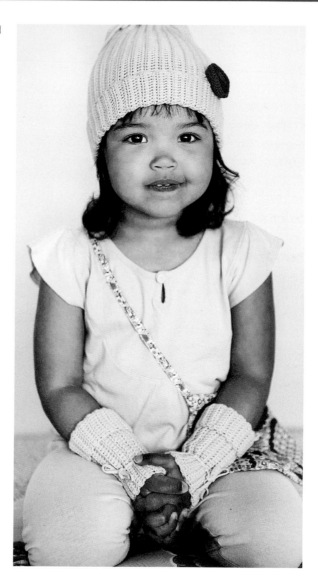

warm when it's colder. These are decorated with little flowers but hearts (*see page 27*) or buttons work just as well. You can buy imitation suede cord in a craft store.

Yarn: CYCA #3 (DK/light worsted) Sandnes Duo (55% Merino wool, 45% cotton, 136 yd/124 m / 50 g; *see page 142*)

Yarn Amounts: Approx. 50 g

Crochet Hook: U.S. size H-8 / 5 mm

Notions: Imitation suede cord

NOTE: Hold yarn double throughout.

With two strands of yarn held together, ch 9.

Row 1: Beginning in 2nd ch from hook, work 1 sc in each st across; turn.

Rows 2-21: Ch 1, 1 sc through back loop of each st across; turn.

After working 21 rows, fold the wrist warmer with RS facing RS, aligning edges, and join with sc through both layers. Cut yarn and draw end through last st.

Now the ribbing is complete. Turn the cuff and work 21 dc spaced evenly around. Substitute ch 2 for the 1st dc of each round and end each rnd with 1 sl st into top of ch 2. Work 9 rnds of dc (or length to fit). Cut yarn and draw end through last st; weave in ends on WS.

The wrist warmers shown in the photo are finished with a "Simple flower 1," (*see instructions on page 22*) and an imitation suede cord threaded through the sts of the ribbing.

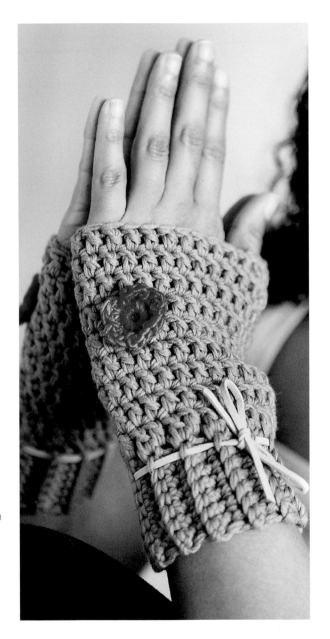

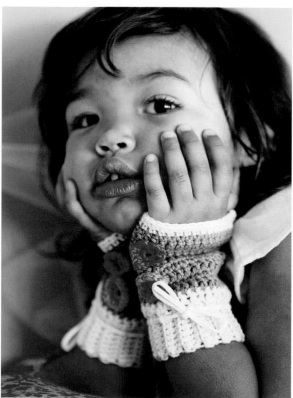

WRIST WARMERS FOR CHILDREN

Sizes: small child (large child)

Yarn: CYCA #3 (DK/light worsted) Sandnes Duo (55% Merino wool, 45% cotton, 136 yd/124 m / 50 g; *see page 142*)

Yarn Amounts: 50 g of each color

Crochet Hook: U.S. size E-4 / 3.5 mm

Notions: Imitation suede cord

Ch 9 (10).

Row 1: Beginning in 2nd ch from hook, work 1 sc in each st across; turn.

Rows 2–25 (2–30): Ch 1, 1 sc through back loop of each st across; turn.

Fold the wrist warmer with RS facing RS, aligning edges, and join with sc through both layers. Cut yarn and draw end through last st.

Now the ribbing is complete. Turn the cuff and work 30 (32) dc spaced evenly around. Substitute ch 2 for the 1st dc of each round and end each rnd with 1 sl st into top of ch 2. Rounds with sc begin with ch 1 and end with 1 sl st into 1st ch.

Change colors and alternate 1 rnd dc, 1 rnd sc. Work approx. 10 (13) rounds this way or until desired length. End by working 2 rnds sc in the same color as the ribbing.

The wrist warmers shown in the photo are finished with a "Simple flower 1," (*see instructions on page 22*) and an imitation suede cord threaded through the sts of the ribbing.

Wrapped sweater, adult size

Crocheted garments are very popular right now and decorated sweaters get top billing.

A crocheted sweater is a large project designed for anyone with some crochet experience or who wants a challenge. The pattern itself isn't too difficult. The entire sweater is made with double crochet in one piece, beginning at the left sleeve, continuing to the back and front, and ending with the right sleeve.

Sizes: S (M, L, XL)

Finished Measurements

Chest: 36 (40¼, 43, 48) in / 91.5 (102,109, 122) cm

Length: 20 (21, 21¾, 22¾) in / 51 (53.5, 55, 58) cm

Yarn: CYCA #3 (DK/light worsted) Sandnes Duo (55% Merino wool, 45% cotton, 136 yd/124 m / 50 g; *see page 142*)

Yarn Amounts: 650 (700, 700, 750) g MC + 50 g CC for edgings

Crochet Hook: U.S. size D-3 / 3 mm

Gauge: 22 dc x 13 rows = 4 x 4 in / 10 x 10 cm

LEFT SLEEVE

Ch 70 (76, 84, 90).

Row 1: Ch 3 (= 1st dc), 1 dc in 5th ch from hook and then 1 dc in each ch across; turn.

Rows 2-52: Ch 3 (= 1st dc), 1 dc in 2nd st and each st to end of row; turn.

After completing Row 52, ch 74 (77, 77, 80).

BACK AND LEFT FRONT

Row 1: Ch 3 (= 1st dc), 1 dc in 5th ch from hook and then 1 dc in each st across until 2-3 sts before end of row. Remove hook from loop and insert it in the top of on the last dc row of left sleeve (at top of ch 3 at beginning of row). With another ball of yarn, make 1 sl st and then ch 74 (77, 77, 80). Cut yarn and draw end through last st. Now insert hook into the st that it was in before you made the sl st and continue in dc to end of row (including the new chain sts); turn = 218 (230, 238, 250) sts.

Rows 2-18: Ch 3 (= 1st dc), 1 dc in 2nd st and each st to end of row; turn.

BACK

Row 1: Ch 3 (= 1st dc), 1 dc in each st to end of back = 111 (117, 121, 127) sts.

Rows 2-22: Work as for Row 1. Do not cut yarn but leave the last loop open so you can return to it later.

LEFT FRONT

Insert hook into dc at top left of the last dc made on Row 1 of back. With RS facing you and a new ball of yarn, draw up a loop.

Row 1: Ch 3 (= 1st dc), 1 dc in each st to end of front = 111 (117, 121, 127) sts.

Rows 2-16: Work as for Row 1.

At the same time, shape the neck, beginning on Row 1, as follows: Decrease 1 st with dc2tog (= *yarn around hook,

hook through next st, yarn around hook and through st, yarn around hook and through 2 loops on hook*; repeat from * to * and then yarn around hook and through rem

3 loops) at neck edge on every other row 16 times. Cut yarn and draw end through last st at end of Row 16.

RIGHT FRONT

Ch 70 (72, 72, 74).

Row 1: Ch 3 (= 1st dc), 1 dc in 5th ch from hook and then 1 dc in each st across.

Rows 2-24: Work as for Row 1.

At the same time, shape the neck, beginning on Row 2, as follows: Increase 1 st with 2 dc into 1 st at neck edge on every other row 9 times and then on every row 16 (18, 20, 22) times. Cut yarn and draw end through last st at end of Row 16.

BACK AND RIGHT FRONT

Row 1: Insert hook into the loop you leave on the back, ch 3 (= 1st dc), work 1 dc in each st across; turn = 218 (230, 238, 250) sts.

Rows 2-18: Ch 3 (= 1st dc), 1 dc in 2nd st and each st to end of row; turn. After completing Row 18, cut yarn and draw end through last st.

RIGHT SLEEVE

Work 1 dc in each of the center 70 (76, 84, 90) sts for 54 rows. Cut yarn and draw end through last st.

FINISHING

Seam the sides and sleeves.

CUFF EDGINGS

Rnd 1: Work in sc evenly spaced around end of sleeve and end with 1 sl st into 1st sc. Make sure you have a multiple of 3 sts.

Rnd 2: Ch 1, (3 dc in next st, 1 sc in each of next 2 sts) around; end with 1 sl st into 1st ch. Cut yarn and draw end through last st.

EDGING AROUND NECK AND BODY OF SWEATER

Row 1: Work in sc around the body, ending with 1 sl st into 1st st; turn. Make sure you have a multiple of 2 sts.

Row 2: Work as for Row 1.

Row 3: Ch 1, (3 dc in next st, 1 sl st) around. Cut yarn and draw end through last st. Weave in all ends on WS.

TIE

Make the tie by working 5 sc along edge of sweater (see photo). Work 5 sc back and forth until the tie is long enough to knot—here, it is approx. 12¾ in / 32 cm long. Finish by sewing on a few flowers, for example, "Simple flowers 1-3" (*see instructions on page 22*).

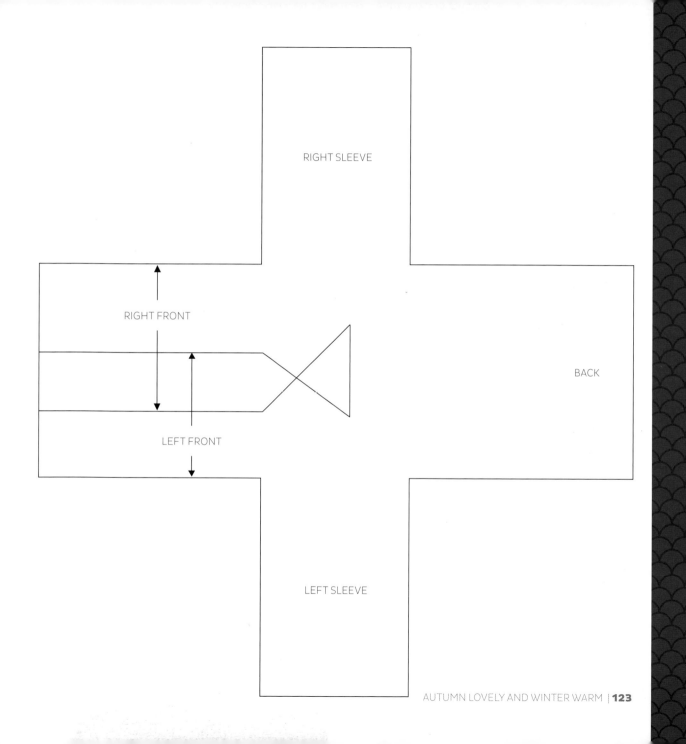

RIGHT SLEEVE

RIGHT FRONT

LEFT FRONT

BACK

LEFT SLEEVE

Crocheted rabbit

Could there be anything sweeter than this rabbit? A cuddly and fun best friend for any kid!

Yarn: CYCA #3 (DK/light worsted) Sandnes Duo (55% Merino wool, 45% cotton, 136 yd/124 m / 50 g; *see page 142*)

Yarn Amounts: 200 g Light Gray 6030 and 50 g each of Pink 2 4616, Light Pink 4312, and Lilac 4823

Crochet Hook: U.S. size G-6 / 4 mm

Notions: 2 safety eyes; fiberfill

NOTES: Hold yarn double throughout. End every rnd with 1 sl st into 1st st.

HEAD

With two strands of Light Gray yarn held together, ch 4 and join into a ring with 1 sl st in 1st ch.

Rnd 1: Ch 1, 6 sc around ring = 6 sts.

Rnd 2: Ch 1, 2 sc in each st around = 12 sts.

Rnd 3: Ch 1, (1 sc in next st, 2 sc in next st) around = 18 sts.

Rnd 4: Ch 1, (1 sc in each of next 2 sts, 2 sc in next st) around = 24 sts.

Rnd 5: Ch 1, (1 sc in each of next 3 sts, 2 sc in next st) around = 30 sts.

Rnd 6: Ch 1, (1 sc in each of next 4 sts, 2 sc in next st) around = 36 sts.

Rnd 7: Ch 1, (1 sc in each of next 5 sts, 2 sc in next st) around = 42 sts.

Rnd 8: Ch 1, (1 sc in each of next 6 sts, 2 sc in next st)

around = 48 sts.

Rnd 9: Ch 1, (1 sc in each of next 7 sts, 2 sc in next st) around = 54 sts.

Rnds 10-15: Ch 1, 1 sc in each st around = 54 sts.

Rnd 16: Ch 1, (1 sc in each of next 7 sts, sc2tog (=insert hook into next st, yarn around hook and through st, hook through next st, yarn around hook and through st = 3 loops on hook; yarn around hook and through all 3 loops at once) around = 48 sts rem.

Rnd 17: Ch 1, (1 sc in each of next 6 sts, sc2tog) = 42 sts rem.

Rnd 18: Ch 1, (1 sc in each of next 5 sts, sc2tog) = 36 sts rem.

Rnd 19: Ch 1, (1 sc in each of next 4 sts, sc2tog) = 30 sts rem.

Rnd 20: Ch 1, (1 sc in each of next 3 sts, sc2tog) = 24 sts rem.

Rnd 21: Ch 1, (1 sc in each of next 2 sts, sc2tog) = 18 sts rem.

Cut yarn and draw end through last st. Securely attach safety eyes. You need to place the eyes before stuffing the head.

BODY

With two strands of Light Gray yarn held together, ch 4 and join into a ring with 1 sl st in 1st ch.

Rnd 1: Ch 1, 6 sc around ring = 6 sts.

Rnd 2: Ch 1, 2 sc in each st around = 12 sts.

Rnd 3: Ch 1, (1 sc in next st, 2 sc in next st) around = 18 sts.

Rnd 4: Ch 1, (1 sc in each of next 2 sts, 2 sc in next st) around = 24 sts.

Rnd 5: Ch 1, (1 sc in each of next 3 sts, 2 sc in next st) around = 30 sts.

Rnd 6: Ch 1, (1 sc in each of next 4 sts, 2 sc in next st) around = 36 sts.

Rnd 7: Ch 1, (1 sc in each of next 5 sts, 2 sc in next st) around = 42 sts.

Rnds 8–11: Ch 1, work 1 sc in each st around = 42 sts.

Rnd 12: Change to Light Pink. Ch 1, work 1 sc in each st around = 42 sts.

Rnd 13: Ch 1, work 1 sc in each st around = 42 sts.

Rnd 14: Change to Pink 2. Ch 1, (work 1 sc in each of next 11 sts, sc2tog) 3 times, sc to end of rnd = 39 sts rem.

Rnd 15: Ch 1, work 1 sc in each st around = 39 sts.

Rnd 16: Change to Light Pink. Ch 1, (work 1 sc in each of next 10 sts, sc2tog) 3 times, sc to end of rnd = 36 sts rem.

Rnd 17: Ch 1, work 1 sc in each st around = 36 sts.

Rnd 18: Change to Pink 2. Ch 1, (work 1 sc in each of next 9 sts, sc2tog) 3 times, sc to end of rnd = 33 sts rem.

Rnd 19: Ch 1, work 1 sc in each st around = 33 sts.

Rnd 20: Change to Light Pink. Ch 1, (work 1 sc in each of next 8 sts, sc2tog) 3 times, sc to end of rnd = 30 sts rem.

Rnd 21: Ch 1, work 1 sc in each st around = 30 sts.

Rnd 22: Change to Pink 2. Ch 1, (work 1 sc in each of next 7 sts, sc2tog) 3 times, sc to end of rnd = 27 sts rem.

Rnd 23: Ch 1, work 1 sc in each st around = 27 sts.

Rnd 24: Change to Light Pink. Ch 1, (work 1 sc in each of next 6 sts, sc2tog) 3 times, sc to end of rnd = 24 sts rem.

Rnd 25: Ch 1, work 1 sc in each st around = 24 sts.

Rnd 26: Change to Pink 2. Ch 1, (work 1 sc in each of next 5 sts, sc2tog) 3 times, sc to end of rnd = 21 sts rem.

Rnd 27: Ch 1, work 1 sc in each st around = 21 sts.

Rnd 28: Change to Light Pink. Ch 1, (work 1 sc in each of next 4 sts, sc2tog) 3 times, sc to end of rnd = 18 sts rem.

Rnd 29: Ch 1, work 1 sc in each st around = 18 sts. Cut yarn and draw end through last st.

DRESS

Rnd 1: Insert hook into the round on the body where you first changed colors from Light Gray to Light Pink. Beginning with Pink 2, ch 1 and work 1 sc in each st around = 42 sts.

Rnd 2: Ch 1, (1 sc, 2 sc in next st) around = 63 sts.

Rnd 3: Change to Light Pink. ch 1, 1 sc in each st around = 63 sts.

Rnd 4: Ch 1, increase 6 sts evenly spaced around = 69 sts.

Rnd 5: Change to Pink 2. Ch 1, 1 sc in each st around = 69 sts.

Rnd 6: Ch 1, 1 sc in each st around = 69 sts.

Rnd 7: Change to Light Pink. Ch 1, 1 sc in each st around = 69 sts.

Rnd 8: Ch 1, 1 sc in each st around = 69 sts.

Rnd 9: Change to Pink 2. Ch 1, (work 3 sc in same st, 1 sl st in each of next 2 sts) around. Cut yarn and draw end through last st.

ARMS

Make 2 arms alike. Begin with Lilac. Ch 4 and join into a ring with 1 sl st in 1st ch.

Rnd 1: Ch 1, 6 sc around ring = 6 sts.

Rnd 2: Ch 1, 2 sc in each st around = 12 sts.

Rnd 3: Ch 1, (1 sc in next st, 2 sc in next st) around = 18 sts.

Rnd 4: Ch 1, (1 sc in each of next 2 sts, 2 sc in next st)

around = 24 sts.

Rnd 5: Ch 1, (1 sc in each of next 2 sts, sc2tog) around = 18 sts rem.

Rnd 6: Ch 1, (1 sc, sc2tog) around = 12 sts rem.

Rnd 7: Change to Light Gray. Ch 1, 1 sc in each st around = 12 sts.

Rnds 8–27: Ch 1, 1 sc in each st around = 12 sts. Cut yarn and draw end through last st after completing Rnd 27.

LEGS

Make 2 legs alike. Begin with Lilac. Ch 4 and join into a ring with 1 sl st in 1st ch.

Rnd 1: Ch 1, 6 sc around ring = 6 sts.

Rnd 2: Ch 1, 2 sc in each st around = 12 sts.

Rnd 3: Ch 1, (1 sc in next st, 2 sc in next st) around = 18 sts.

Rnd 4: Ch 1, (1 sc in each of next 2 sts, 2 sc in next st) around = 24 sts.

Rnds 5–6: Ch 1, 1 sc in each st around = 24 sts.

Rnd 7: Ch 1, (1 sc in each of next 2 sts, sc2tog) around = 18 sts rem.

Rnd 8: Ch 1, (1 sc in each of next 7 sts, sc2tog) around = 16 sts rem.

Rnd 9: Change to Light Gray. Ch 1, 1 sc in each st around = 16 sts.

Rnds 10–23: Ch 1, 1 sc in each st around = 16 sts. Cut yarn and draw end through last st after completing Rnd 23.

EARS

Make 2 ears alike. With Light Gray, ch 4 and join into a ring with 1 sl st in 1st ch.

Rnd 1: Ch 1, 6 sc around ring = 6 sts.

Rnd 2: Ch 1, 2 sc in each st around = 12 sts.

Rnds 3–14: Ch 1, 1 sc in each st around = 12 sts. Cut yarn and draw end through last st after completing Rnd 14. For our rabbit here, the ears were folded at the center and sewn securely to the head.

NOSE

Make nose with Light Pink yarn. Ch 7.

Row 1: Beginning in 2nd ch from hook, work 1 sc in each ch = 6 sts; turn.

Row 2: Ch 1, sc across = 6 sts; turn.

Row 3: Ch 1, (sc2tog) 3 times; turn = 3 sts rem.

Row 4: Ch 1, sc3tog. Cut yarn and draw end through last st.

Sew nose securely to head. Embroider on the mouth with a few stitches.

DRESS POCKET

Make the pocket with Lilac.

Ch 4 and join into a ring with 1 sl st in 1st ch.

Rnd 1: Ch 1, 6 sc around ring = 6 sts. Do not join end of round.

Row 2: Ch 1, 2 sc in each st across; turn.

Row 3: Ch 1, (1 sc, 2 sc in next st) across.

Row 4: Ch 1, work 8 sc evenly spaced across the top of the pocket. Cut yarn and draw end through last st. Securely sew the pocket at center front of the dress, joining around except for the top which should be left open.

BOW

Make the bow with pink yarn. Ch 10.

Row 1: Beginning in 2nd ch from hook, work 1 sc in each ch across = 9 sts.

Rows 2–5: Ch 1, 1 sc in each st across = 9 sts. Cut yarn and draw end through last st after completing Row 5. With a little Pink 2, wrap the center of the bow and sew securely to one of the rabbit's ears.

FINISHING

Weave in all ends on WS. Fill all the parts of the rabbit with fiberfill. Only fill the lower section of the legs and arm. Sew the head securely to the body and then sew on the legs. Sew the arms along center back, directly below the head.

It's Christmas Time Again

CHRISTMAS IS THE NICEST AND BUSIEST TIME OF THE YEAR and conducive to all kinds of projects. Why not crochet the tree decorations, a Christmas tree rug, or cute little elf hats for the children?

Christmas tree rug

Here's an unusual Christmas tree rug that can be also used for the rest of the year. It is crocheted with tricot rags from recycled clothing. Because it can vary a lot in thickness and elasticity, it is difficult to know for certain how much you need to increase to make the rug flat. (*See the picture on page 128.*)

Yarn: Tricot (stretch knit) rags (Hooked Zpagetti)
Crochet Hook: U.S. size N/P-15 or P/Q / 12 mm (Note: there is no exact U.S. equivalent to 12 mm)
NOTES: Crochet as loosely as possible. End every rnd with 1 sl st into 1ˢᵗ st.

Ch 5 and join into a ring with 1 sl st in 1ˢᵗ ch.
Rnd 1: Ch 1, 8 sc around ring = 8 sts.
Rnd 2: Ch 1, 2 sc in each st around = 16 sts.
Rnd 3: Ch 1, (1 sc in next st, 2 sc in next st) around = 24 sts.
Rnd 4: Ch 1, (1 sc in each of next 2 sts, 2 sc in next st) around = 32 sts.
Rnd 5: Ch 1, (1 sc in each of next 3 sts, 2 sc in next st) around = 40 sts.
Rnd 6: Ch 1, (1 sc in each of next 4 sts, 2 sc in next st) around = 48 sts.
Now you can see how the rug is working out with the thickness of the tricot rags you have.
If the rug starts to ripple, work another 1 or 2 rounds without increasing. If it buckles in, continue increasing.

The instructions below suggest how to proceed with the rug.
Rnds 7–8: Ch 1, 1 sc in each st around = 48 sts.
Rnd 9: Ch 1, (1 sc in each of next 5 sts, 2 sc in next st) around = 56 sts.
Rnd 10: Ch 1, 1 sc in each st around = 56 sts.
Rnd 11: Ch 1, (1 sc in each of next 6 sts, 2 sc in next st) around = 64 sts.
Rnd 12: Ch 1, 1 sc in each st around = 64 sts.
Rnd 13: Ch 1, (1 sc in each of next 7 sts, 2 sc in next st) around = 72 sts.
Rnd 14: Ch 1, 1 sc in each st around = 72 sts.
Rnd 15: Ch 1, (1 sc in each of next 8 sts, 2 sc in next st) around = 80 sts.
Rnd 16: Ch 1, (1 sc in each of next 9 sts, 2 sc in next st) around = 88 sts.
Rnd 17: Ch 1, (1 sc in each of next 10 sts, 2 sc in next st) around = 96 sts.
Rnd 18: Ch 1, (1 sc in each of next 11 sts, 2 sc in next st) around = 104 sts.
Rnd 19: Ch 1, (1 sc in each of next 12 sts, 2 sc in next st) around = 112 sts.
Rnd 20: Ch 1, (1 sc in each of next 13 sts, 2 sc in next st) around = 120 sts.
Rnd 21: Ch 1, (1 sc in each of next 14 sts, 2 sc in next st) around = 128 sts.
Rnd 22: Ch 1, (1 sc in each of next 15 sts, 2 sc in next st) around = 136 sts.

Rnd 23: Ch 1, (1 sc in each of next 16 sts, 2 sc in next st) around = 144 sts.

Rnd 24: Ch 1, (1 sc in each of next 17 sts, 2 sc in next st) around = 152 sts.

The next two rounds describe how to make an edging for the rug. If you want a larger rug, just continue increasing.

Rnd 25: Ch 6, skip 5 sts and work 1 sc in next st, (ch 7, skip 6 sts, 1 sc in next st) 20 times and end with ch 6, skip 5 sts, 1 sc in next st; 1 sl st in 1st ch.

Rnd 26 (Flower petals): In every ch loop, work (1 sc, 6 dc, 1 sc). End with 1 sl st in 1st sc. Cut yarn and draw end through last st.

Because it is very difficult to thread the tricot for weaving in, knot all loose ends on WS to secure them.

Christmas potholders

CHRISTMASSY POTHOLDER

Yarn: CYCA #1 (sock/fingering/baby) Mandarin Petit (100% cotton, 195 yd/178 m / 50 g; *see page 142*)

Yarn Amounts: Leftover yarns in desired colors

Crochet Hook: U.S. size G-6 / 4 mm

NOTE: Hold yarn double throughout.

With two strands of yarn held together, ch 4 and join into a ring with 1 sl st in 1st ch.

End every rnd with 1 sl st into 1st ch on rounds with single crochet and to top of ch 2 on double crochet rounds.

Rnd 1: Ch 2 (= 1st dc), work 11 dc around ring.

Rnd 2: Ch 2, 1 dc in same space, 2 dc in each space between dc around = 12 dc groups.

Rnd 3: Ch 2, 2 dc into same space, (3 dc in each space between dc groups of previous rnd) around = 12 groups.

Rnd 4: Ch 1, (1 sc into each of next 2 sts, 2 sc in next st) around.

Rnd 5: Ch 2, 1 dc in each st around.

Rnd 6: Ch 1, (1 sc into each of next 3 sts, 2 sc in next st) around.

Rnd 7: Ch 1, (1 sc into each of next 4 sts, 2 sc in next st) around

Rnd 8 (edging): Ch 1, (3 dc in next st, 2 sl st) around. Ch a cord as long as you like for the hanging loop, join with 1 sl st into 1st ch to form a loop, and work 1 sl st into each ch and into join. Cut yarn and draw end through last st. Weave in all ends on WS.

STAR POTHOLDER

This potholder is crocheted with doubled yarn so it is really big. If you want a smaller potholder, use a single strand of yarn and the pattern will work just as well. If the potholder is a little "bubbly" when it is finished, no problem—spray it with water and pat it out flat or steam press gently.

Yarn: CYCA #1 (sock/fingering/baby) Mandarin Petit (100% cotton, 195 yd/178 m / 50 g; see page 142)

Yarn Amounts: Leftover yarns in desired colors

Crochet Hook: U.S. size E-4 / 3.5 mm

NOTE: Hold yarn double throughout.

With two strands of yarn held together, ch 5 and join into a ring with 1 sl st into 1st ch.

Rnd 1: Ch 4 (= 1 dc + 2 ch), (1 dc around ring, ch 2) 7 times and end with 1 sl st into 2nd ch at beginning of rnd.

Rnd 2: Ch 2, 1 dc in 1st ch loop of previous rnd, ch 2, (2 dc in next ch loop, ch 2) around; end with 1 sl st into 1st ch.

Rnd 3: Ch 2, 1 dc in sl st, 1 dc, (ch 2, 2 dc in next st, 1 dc) around and end with ch 2 and 1 sl st into 1st ch.

Rnd 4: Ch 2, 1 dc in sl st, 1 dc in next st, 2 dc in next st, (ch 2, 2 dc in next st, 1 dc, 2 dc in next st) around and end with ch 2 and 1 sl st into 1st ch.

Rnd 5: Ch 2, 1 dc in sl st, 3 dc, 2 dc in next st, (ch 2, 2 dc in next st, 1 dc in each of next 3 dc, 2 dc in next st) around and end with ch 2 and 1 sl st into 1st ch.

Rnd 6: Ch 2, 1 dc in sl st, 5 dc, 2 dc in next st, (ch 2, 2 dc in next st, 1 dc in each of next 5 dc, 2 dc in next st) around and end with ch 2 and 1 sl st into 1st ch.

Rnd 7: Ch 2, 1 dc in sl st, 7 dc, 2 dc in next st, (ch 2, 2 dc in next st, 1 dc in each of next 7 dc, 2 dc in next st) around and end with ch 2 and 1 sl st into 1st ch.

Rnd 8: 1 sl st, ch 2, 8 dc, ch 2, 2 dc around ch loop, ch 2, (skip 1st of star, 9 dc, ch 2, 2 dc around ch loop, ch 2) around and end with 1 sl st into 1st sl st.

NOTE: In the following rounds, * = work sts around next chain loop.

Rnd 9: 1 sl st, ch 2, 6 dc, ch 2, 2 dc around ch loop, ch 2, 2 dc*, ch 2, (skip 1st of star, 7 dc, ch 2, 2 dc*, ch 2, 2 dc, ch 2) around and end with 1 sl st into 1st sl st.

Rnd 10: 1 sl st, ch 2, 4 dc, ch 2, 2 dc around ch loop, ch 2, 2 dc*, ch 2, 2 dc*, ch 2, (skip 1st of star, 5 dc, ch 2, 2 dc*, ch 2, 2 dc*, ch 2, 2 dc*, ch 2) around and end with 1 sl st into 1st sl st.

Rnd 11: 1 sl st, ch 2, 2 dc, ch 2, 2 dc around ch loop, ch 2, 2 dc*, ch 2, 2 dc*, ch 2, 2 dc*, ch 2, (skip 1st of star, 3 dc, ch 2, 2 dc*, ch 2, 2 dc*, ch 2, 2 dc*, ch 2, 2 dc*, ch 2) around and end with 1 sl st into 1st sl st.

Rnd 12: 1 sl st, ch 2, 2 dc around ch loop, ch 2, 2 dc*, ch 2, 2 dc*, ch 2, 2 dc*, ch 2, 2 dc*, ch 2 (skip 1st of star, 1 dc, ch 2, 2 dc*, ch 2, 2 dc*, ch 2, 2 dc*, ch 2 , 2 dc*, ch 2, 2 dc*, ch 2) around and end with 1 sl st into 1st sl st.

Set piece aside and make another the same way. The two pieces are then joined with the edging:

Rnd 13: (3 dc in each ch loop, ch 3) around.

Rnd 14: 3 sl sts across 1st 3 dc of previous rnd, then (1 sc, 2 dc, 1 sc) in each ch loop around, ending with 1 sl st into 1st st.

Ch a cord as long as you like for the hanging loop, join with 1 sl st into 1st ch to form a loop, and work 1 sl st into each ch and into join. Cut yarn and draw end through last st. Weave in all ends on WS.

SMALL CHRISTMAS TREE ORNAMENT

Yarn: CYCA #1 (sock/fingering/baby) Mandarin Petit (100% cotton, 195 yd/178 m / 50 g; *see page 142*)

Crochet Hook: U.S. size D-3 / 3 mm

Notions: Fiber fill and small pompoms

Ch 20.

Row 1: Beginning in 3rd ch from hook, work 1 dc in each ch across = 18 sts.

Row 2: Ch 2, dc2tog (= *yarn around hook, hook through next st, yarn around hook and through st, yarn around hook and through 2 loops on hook*; repeat from * to * and then yarn around hook and through rem 3 loops), 14 dc, dc2tog; turn = 16 sts rem.

Row 3: Ch 2, dc2tog, 12 dc, dc2tog; turn = 14 sts rem.

Row 4: Ch 2, dc2tog, 10 dc, dc2tog; turn = 12 sts rem.

Row 5: Ch 2, dc2tog, 8 dc, dc2tog; turn = 10 sts rem.

Row 6: Ch 2, dc2tog, 6 dc, dc2tog; turn = 8 sts rem.

Row 7: Ch 2, dc2tog, 4 dc, dc2tog; turn = 6 sts rem.

Row 8: Ch 2, dc2tog, 2 dc, dc2tog; turn = 4 sts rem.

Row 9: Ch 2, dc2tog, dc2tog; turn = 2 sts rem.

Row 10: Ch 2, dc2tog. Cut yarn and draw end through last last.

Make another tree the same way. Join them: with a contrast color and RS of each piece facing out, work sc through both layers, evenly spaced around. When you've worked around 2 sides of the tree, stop and add a little fiberfill. I also sewed some small pompoms (available from craft shops) on as some "Christmas balls." If you can't find any tiny pompoms, crochet some little circles and sew them on securely. Finish joining the layers; weave in ends to WS. Thread a twisted cord through the top as a hanging loop.

GRANNY STAR

Yarn: CYCA #1 (sock/fingering/baby) Mandarin Petit (100% cotton, 195 yd/178 m / 50 g; *see page 142*)

Crochet Hook: U.S. size C-2 / 2.5 mm for single strand of yarn or G-6 / 4 mm for double yarn

NOTE: If desired, work with yarn held double throughout.

Ch 5 and join into a ring with 1 sl st in 1st ch.

Rnd 1: Work all dc around ring. Ch 2 (= 1st dc), 2 dc, ch 1, (3 dc, ch 1) 4 times and end with 1 sl st into top of ch 2 at beginning of rnd.

Rnd 2: Sl st to space with 1 st from previous rnd, (3 dc, ch 2, 3 dc around ch, ch 1) around and end with 1 sl st to top of ch 3.

Rnd 3: 2 sl sts, (3 dc, ch 2, 3 dc in ch-2 loop, 1 sc in ch-1 loop) around and end with 1 sl st in 1st st.

HEART

Yarn: CYCA #1 (sock/fingering/baby) Mandarin Petit (100% cotton, 195 yd/178 m / 50 g; *see page 142*)

Crochet Hook: U.S. size D-3 / 3 mm

Follow the instructions for the "Large heart" (see page 27).

Christmas garlands

Garlands are very decorative and can be hung up here and there. You can hang some on the tree and some on the mantel.

GARLAND WITH HEARTS

Yarn: CYCA #1 (sock/fingering/baby) Mandarin Petit (100% cotton, 195 yd/178 m / 50 g; *see page 142*)
Crochet Hook: U.S. size C-2 / 2.5 mm

Heart: Ch 4 and join into a ring with 1 sl st into 1st ch.
Rnd 1: Work all dc and tr around ring. Ch 2, 2 tr, 3 dc, ch 1, 1 tr, ch 1, 3 dc, 2 tr, ch 2; end with 1 sl st into top of ch 2.
Rnd 2: Ch 2, 2 sc in each of the next 2 tr, 1 sc in each of the next 3 sts, ch 1, 1 sc in each of the next 6 sts, 2 sc in each of the next 2 sts, ch 2; end with 1 sl st into top of ch 2. Cut yarn and draw end through last st; weave in ends on WS.
Crochet as many hearts as you want for your garland and then decide if you want to string them onto some yarn or a cord, or, as here, make a chain stitch cord between the hearts.
Work 42 ch between each heart and 4 ch down to the top of each heart. Join each heart with 1 sc and then ch 4 back to the cord, joining with 1 sl st into chain to form a loop. Ch 42 to the next heart.

GARLAND WITH FLAG PENNANTS

Yarn: CYCA #1 (sock/fingering/baby) Mandarin Petit (100% cotton, 195 yd/178 m / 50 g; *see page 142*)
Crochet Hook: U.S. size C-2 / 2.5 mm

Ch 16.
Row 1: Beginning in 2nd ch from hook, work 15 sc across; end with ch 1, turn.
Row 2: Work 12 sc, 1 sl st and end with ch 1; turn.
Row 3: Skip the 1st st, 12 sc, and end with ch 1; turn.
Row 4: Work 9 sc, 1 sl st, and end with ch 1; turn.
Row 5: Skip 1st st, 9 sc, and end with ch 1; turn.
Row 6: Work 9 sc, ch 3, and end with ch 1; turn.
Row 7: Work 1 sc in each of the 3 ch, 9 sc across, and end with ch 1; turn.
Row 8: Work 12 sc, ch 2, and end with ch 1; turn.
Row 9: Work 1 sc in each of the 2 ch, 12 sc across. Cut yarn and draw end through last st.
Crochet the crosses on each flag with slip st centered from the top down and across. Weave in all ends on WS. When you've crocheted all the flags you want, spray them with a little water and steam press so they will lie flat. Join them as follows:
Ch 30, join a flag with sc evenly spaced down short end of flag. Ch 20 between each flag and continue until all the flags are joined. End with ch 30. Cut yarn and draw end through last st.

Elf hat

Yarn: CYCA #1 (sock/fingering/baby) Mandarin Petit (100% cotton, 195 yd/178 m / 50 g; *see page 142*)
Yarn Amounts: 100 g White 1001, 100 g Red 4418, 50 g Green 8514
Crochet Hook: U.S. size G-6 / 4 mm
NOTE: Hold yarn double throughout.

End every round with 1 sl st in 1st st to complete round. Switch between Red and White on every 5th rnd. Begin with Red and change to White, for the first color change only, after completing 6 rnds. This hat will fit most children, but if you want a smaller hat, do not increase as much as in the pattern. If you want a larger hat, work more increase rounds.

With two strands of Red held together, ch 4 and join into a ring with 1 sl st in 1st ch. End every rnd with 1 sl st into 1st ch to complete the rnd.
Rnd 1: Ch 1, 6 sc around ring = 6 sts.
Rnd 2: Ch 1, 2 sc in each st around = 12 sts.
Rnds 3–76: Ch 1, 1 sc in each st around = 12 sts. Change colors as indicated above.
Rnd 77: Ch 1, (1 sc in next st, 2 sc in next st) around = 18 sts.
Rnd 78: Ch 1, 1 sc in each st around = 18 sts.
Rnd 79: Ch 1, (1 sc in each of next 2 sts, 2 sc in next st) around = 24 sts.
Rnd 80: Ch 1, 1 sc in each st around = 24 sts.

Rnd 81: Ch 1, (1 sc in each of next 3 sts, 2 sc in next st) around = 30 sts.
Rnd 82: Ch 1, 1 sc in each st around = 30 sts.
Rnd 83: Ch 1, (1 sc in each of next 4 sts, 2 sc in next st) around = 36 sts.
Rnd 84: Ch 1, 1 sc in each st around = 36 sts.
Rnd 85: Ch 1, (1 sc in each of next 5 sts, 2 sc in next st) around = 42 sts.
Rnd 86: Ch 1, 1 sc in each st around = 42 sts.
Rnd 87: Ch 1, (1 sc in each of next 6 sts, 2 sc in next st) around = 48 sts.
Rnd 88: Ch 1, 1 sc in each st around = 48 sts.
Rnd 89: Ch 1, (1 sc in each of next 7 sts, 2 sc in next st) around = 54 sts.
Rnd 90: Ch 1, 1 sc in each st around = 54 sts.
Rnd 91: Ch 1, (1 sc in each of next 8 sts, 2 sc in next st) around = 60 sts.
Rnd 92: Ch 1, 1 sc in each st around = 60 sts.
Rnd 93: Ch 1, (1 sc in each of next 9 sts, 2 sc in next st) around = 66 sts.
Rnd 94: Ch 1, 1 sc in each st around = 66 sts.
Rnd 95: Ch 1, (1 sc in each of next 10 sts, 2 sc in next st) around = 72 sts.
Rnds 96–111: Ch 1, 1 sc in each st around = 72 sts.
Rnds 112–116: Change to Green. Ch 1, 1 sc in each st around = 72 sts.
Last rnd: Change to Red and work crab st all around (= sc worked from left to right).

POMPOM

I attached a large pompom to the tip of the hat. You can easily make a pompom with a pompom maker from the craft store or with 2 circles of stiff paper. Cut out a small circle at the center of each piece, like a doughnut hole. Hold the circles together and wrap the yarn around and around, through the holes—threading yarn onto a tapestry needle makes it easier—until the circles are completely filled. Cut yarn around outer edge and firmly tie a strong thread between the circles and around the ball to secure it. Remove the paper circles and trim ball evenly, but be careful not to trim too much! Steaming also fluffs up the pompom (be sure to protect your hands). Securely sew the pompom to the tip of the hat.

Crochet around metal shapes

You can find metal rods and even metal hearts and stars in various kinds of stores. For this project, I used several sizes of heart. The large heart was covered with moss last Christmas but this year it had a totally different look.

WORK AS FOLLOWS:

I worked in single crochet all around the large heart with tricot (stretch knit) Hooked Zpagetti. I used a hook that was U.S. size N/P-15—P/Q / 12 mm. I alternated the sc from one side of the frame to the door by catching the yarn with the hook from one side for 1 sc and then from the other side for the next sc. Knot ends to fasten off. For the small hearts, I worked with a hook that was U.S. size D-3 / 3 mm and Mandarin Petit (*see page 142*) yarn, working all the sc stitches from the same side of the frame. Cut yarn and draw end through last st. Fasten off the ends or use them to hang the small hearts within a large heart as shown here.

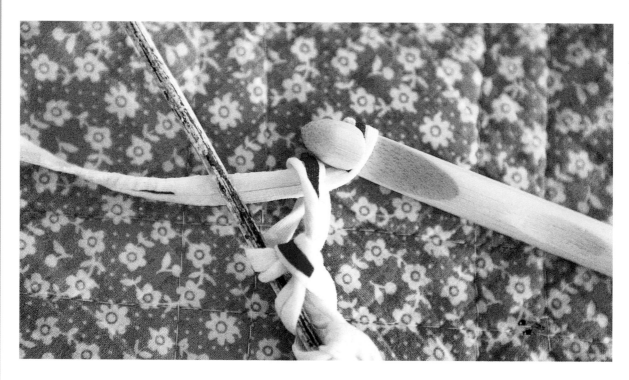

Yarn

The yarns used for the projects in this book are almost exclusively Mandarin Petit and Sandnes Duo. The color numbers are below.

Mandarin Petit (Sandnes Garn)

CYCA #1, 100% COTTON, 195 YD/178 M / 50 G

WHITE	1001
NATURAL WHITE	1002
YELLOW	2315
ORANGE	2709
CORAL	4007
RED	4418
CERISE	4517
PINK	4505
LIGHT PINK	4301
PINK-LILAC	4915
NAVY BLUE	6073
TURQUOISE	6705
LIGHT LILAC	5212
MEDIUM LILAC	5314
DARK LILAC	5226
LIGHT TURQUOISE	6803
LIME	8722
GREEN	8514

Sandnes Duo (Sandnes Garn)

CYCA #3, 55% MERINO WOOL, 45% COTTON, 136 YD/124 M / 50 G

NATURAL WHITE	1002
LIGHT BROWN	244141
DARK BROWN	3161
LIGHT PINK	4312
PINK 1	4515
PINK 2	4616
LILAC	4823
DARK LILAC	4762
RED	4219
PETROLEUM	6534
LIGHT GRAY	6030
DARK GRAY	5873
BLACK	1099
ORANGE	2709

For the projects on pages 34, 42, 48, and 63, we used yarn from another source:
Marks & Kattens Flox (CYCA #3, 100% cotton, 153 yd/140 m / 50 g; Red 4747-1765)

Acknowledgments

I EXTEND MANY WARM THANKS TO EVERYONE WITHOUT WHOM THIS BOOK WOULD NOT HAVE BEEN POSSIBLE.

Leo and Ozzy—my beloved children—thank you for inspiring me and enriching my life; I love you!

Ronnie—my beloved husband who puts up with all my crazy pranks and ideas—thank you for being in my life and understanding my passion and what I fight for; I love you!

Mamma Kerstin—thank you, Mom, for all the help I got even though you have constant pain in your joints. Thank you for teaching me how to crochet, helping me crochet many of the projects in this book, coming up with ideas, and helping with the proofreading. Without you, I would never have been able to produce this book!

Pappa Owe—for general support and taking care of the children along with Mom. Thank you for believing in me, my beloved parents.

Aunt Lisbeth Grandin from the yarn store 2knit. Thank you for your support, good ideas, tips, and contributions of materials for the models in the book.

Petra Setterberg—my well-loved friend, who doesn't just share the happy times with me, but pushes me and listens to my agonies as we go, and who designed such a wonderful layout for my book. You are the best, Petra!

Linda Cibri from the shop Sally Bazar—fantastic Linda not only generously contributed with good ideas and so kindly supported me, she also let me borrow all those many great props from her shop that made my photos so much better. Thank you for all your contributions!

Sandnes Garn—sponsored me with a quantity of fine yarns that made it possible to crochet all the models in the book. Thanks to Birgitta Andersson for your kind responses every time I asked for yarn.

Cotton & Button is the brand of the beautiful night clothes that all of the models in my book posed in. Thank you to Charlotte Persson for lending me your fine garments, which made my crochet pieces look so much nicer.

Anna and Maya Skoglund—you are so fantastic in so many ways and I certainly don't know where to begin or end. I am especially thankful that I got to use you as models in the book. Totally unbelievable to have such talented models as neighbors.

Meja Grankvist—I want to thank you for the phenomenally good work you did as a photo model for one day. You are fantastic!

Malin Magnusson and her daughter Ebba—my littlest model—who made me run around and look for various things for the little sweetpea to hold onto during the photo shoots. Thanks to Malin and Ebba—we worked well together!

Last, but absolutely not least, I want to thank my publisher ICA Bokförlag, and especially my editors, Heidi-Marie Wallinder and Roger Carlson, who believed in me and supported me all along the way in this fun and, for me, totally new project.

SUPPLIER INFORMATION:

Nordic Yarn Imports (US Distributor)
Swedish Yarn Imports
PO Box 2069
Jamestown, NC 27282
800-331-5648
www.swedishyarn.com
info@swedishyarn.com

Webs – America's Yarn Store
75 Service Center Road
Northampton, M A 01060
800-367-9327
www.yarn.com
customerservice@yarn.com

If you are unable to obtain any of the yarn used in this book, it can be replaced with a yarn of a similar weight and composition. Please note, however, that the finished projects may vary slightly from those shown, depending on the yarn used. Try www.yarnsub.com for suggestions.
For more information on selecting or substituting yarn, contact your local yarn shop or an online store; they are familiar with all types of yarns and would be happy to help you. Additionally, the online knitting community at Ravelry.com has forums where you can post questions about specific yarns. Yarns come and go so quickly these days and there are so many beautiful yarns available.

Continued from page 103

Row 6: Work 1 sc into each of next 7 sts, 2 sc in next st, 1 sc, 2 sc in next st, 1 sc in each of next 7 sts; end with ch 1 and turn = 19 sts.

OUTER EAR (WHITE)

With U.S. size G-6 / 4 mm hook and two strands of yarn held together, ch 4 and join into a ring with 1 sl st into 1st ch.

Row 1: Ch 1, 7 sc around ring; end with 1 sl st into 1st ch; turn = 7 sts.

Row 2: Work 1 sc into each of next 3 sts, 3 sc into next st, 1 sc into each of next 3 sts and end with ch 1 and turn = 9 sts.

Row 3: Work 1 sc into each of next 4 sts, 3 sc into next st, 1 sc in each of next 4 sts; end with ch 1 and turn = 11 sts.

Row 4: Work (1 sc, 2 sc in next sc, 1 sc in each of next 2 sts, 2 sc in next sc) twice; 1 sc; end with ch 1 and turn = 15 sts.

Row 5: Work 1 sc into each of next 6 sts, 2 sc in next st, 1 sc, 2 sc in next st, 1 sc in each of next 6 sts; end with ch 1 and turn = 17 sts.

Row 6: Work 1 sc into each of next 7 sts, 2 sc in next st, 1 sc, 2 sc in next st, 1 sc in each of next 7 sts; end with ch 1 and turn = 19 sts.

Row 7: Sc across row = 19 sts; cut yarn and draw end through last st. Sew ear parts together and then sew on ears placed as shown in photo. Weave in all ends on WS.

Continued from page 115

Rnd 1: Ch 1, work 6 sc around ring. End with 1 sl st into 1st ch.

Rnd 2: Ch 2, work 1 dc in same space as ch 2 and then work 2 dc in each st around; end with 1 sl st into top of ch 2 at beginning of rnd.

CIRCLE 3

Ch 4 and join into a ring with 1 sl st into 1st ch.

Rnd 1: Ch 2 (= 1st dc), work 11 dc around ring. End with 1 sl st into top of ch 2 at beginning of rnd.

Rnd 2: Ch 2, work 1 dc in same space as ch 2 and then work 2 dc in each st around; end with 1 sl st into top of ch 2 at beginning of rnd.

Rnd 3: Ch 2, and then alternate (2 dc in next st, 1 dc in next) around. End with 1 sl st into top of ch 2 at beginning of rnd.